WHO SHOULD BE HELPED?

Volume 83, Sage Library of Social Research

Sage Library of Social Research

WHO SHOULD BE HELPED?

Public Support for Social Services

FAY LOMAX COOK

Foreword by Theodore R. Marmor

Volume 83
SAGE LIBRARY OF
SOCIAL RESEARCH

 SAGE PUBLICATIONS   Beverly Hills   London

For information address:

SAGE PUBLICATIONS, INC.
275 South Beverly Drive
Beverly Hills, California 90212

SAGE PUBLICATIONS LTD
28 Banner Street
London EC1Y 8QE England

Printed in the United States of America

Library of Congress Cataloging in Publication Data

Cook, Fay Lomax.
  Who should be helped?

  (Sage library of social research ; v. 83)
  Bibliography: p.
  Includes index.
  1. Public welfare--United States. 2. Public
welfare--United States--Citizen participation.
3. United States--Social policy. I. Title.
HV95.C648   361.6'2'0973   79-12619
ISBN 0-8039-1135-1
ISBN 0-8039-1136-X pbk.

FIRST PRINTING

DEDICATION

This book is dedicated to my best friend and husband
Thomas Dixon Cook, without whose enthusiastic encouragement and active help, I would never have finished this book.

And it is also dedicated to our son
David Robert Lomax Cook, without whose entry into the world May 29, 1978, I might have finished the book earlier. However, the moments free of work would not have been so filled with joy and discovery.

CONTENTS

ACKNOWLEDGMENTS

The research reported here was supported by the Administration on Aging under grant 90-A-524. For their help and encouragement, I am indebted to Byron Gold, Associate Commissioner for Education and Training, Administration on Aging; and Kenneth Prewitt, Director, National Opinion Research Center, Chicago. I am also grateful to Calvin Jones and Robert Shapiro, research assistants at the National Opinion Research Center, who provided superbly capable help in data analysis as well as useful comments throughout the study. Also providing helpful comments on earlier drafts of selected chapters of the manuscript were Constance E. Kellam, Associate Professor, Loyola University School of Social Work; Elizabeth A. Kutza, Assistant Professor, University of Chicago School of Social Service Administration; Donnel M. Pappenfort, Professor, University of Chicago School of Social Service Administration; and Sheldon S. Tobin, Associate Professor, University of Chicago School of Social Service Administration.

Five other people deserve very special thanks. First, I owe Theodore R. Marmor, Professor, Political Science Department, and Director, Center for Health Studies, Yale University, a large debt of gratitude. Without his very special help and support, I might not have embarked on a study of this magnitude. Second, Albert Erlebacher, Associate Professor, Psychology Department, Northwestern University, spent many hours helping me develop the experimental design which is embedded within the survey. Without his particular skills and creativity, I would not have been able to include such a complex design. Third, Rosalind B. Forrest typed several drafts of the manuscript cheerfully and intelligently. Without her help, the final stages of the book would have been much more difficult. Fourth, Susan J. Cahill prepared the index and helped in numerous other ways. Her calm in the face of deadlines and her unflusterable good humor were important contributions. Finally, and with most heartfelt thanks, I acknowledge my husband, Thomas D. Cook, Professor, Psychology Department, Northwestern University, who has provided advice and help at every stage of this endeavor from conception to final write-up. This book is dedicated to him.

– F. L. C.

FOREWORD

Fay Cook's book is about American views of the welfare state. Her materials are the beliefs, attitudes, and values of a Chicago population she surveyed in 1976-1977. And her achievement is a careful analysis of the grounds on which Americans are willing to support programs redistributing aid to particular social groups. As such, Cook's work substantially advances the understanding of public opinion and the American welfare state.

The striking fact about the contemporary welfare state is the similarity of concerns across national borders in North America and Western Europe. The level of economic growth, environmental abuses, the trend toward a more elderly society, and the shape of social welfare programs—these reappear as the categories of discussion about the future of the welfare state.

The oil crisis of the early 1970s dramatized the difficulty all the Western industrial states face in maintaining postwar rates of economic growth. The image of a steadily expanding national pie is almost everywhere challenged. American budget officials, for instance, expected growth rates between five and six percent for the 1975-1980 period and forecast GNP increases of about three percent per year by the early 1980s. Further, worker productivity is expected to increase by only one percent per year, about half the historical American average. The availability of national fiscal resources for welfare state outlays is as a result increasingly a matter of worry.

At the same time, environmental issues press upon both the availability of resources and the rates of economic growth. Concerns about cleaner air, less polluted waters, safer working environments, and less degraded physical settings mean pressure on the prices of goods and services and increased competition for public funds devoted to citizen welfare. The conflict between economic dislocation and the environment—stark over issues like the location of nuclear power plants—emerges everywhere.

A third force of change is simply the demographic alteration of Western industrial societies. The most prominent element is the aging of these societies: the steady reduction of the ratio of workers to nonworkers as birth rates fall, longevity increases, and retirement occurs earlier. Particularly crucial for this book is the anticipated increases in the numbers of old elderly, those over seventy-five who make predictably large claims upon pension benefits, medical care, and special social services. The concern about the old is not, as with forecasts of lower birth rates, subject to sudden shifts. The old of the year 2000 are already alive; short of catastrophe, the age distribution of the end of the century will likely follow the forecasts with great reliability. As the number of claimants increases, the strain on budgets promotes review of the structure and levels of social programs, particularly those in health, pensions, and the personal social services.

Forecasted strains have already inspired programmatic review. Income support programs started much earlier typically expanded their coverage to include a larger proportion of the general population. Among the factors creating these margins for expansion were rapid economic growth with relatively stable prices, an abundance of readily exploitable natural resources and primary products, and public fiscal resources freed up by the absence of severe unemployment. These margins began to fill up by the mid-1970s. Interstices between income support programs and private contracts, taxa-

tion and other social programs have narrowed appreciably.
The frontiers of policy development no longer stretch toward
a horizon of unimpeded growth and cheap resources, but are
now internal frontiers constrained by difficult trade-offs.

These are among the main elements of strain within the
contemporary welfare state. And it is in that broader context
that Fay Cook's careful scholarship makes a special contribution. Her subject is not the welfare state and its overall
character, but what citizens think of it. As her opening
chapter clearly states, the precise subject is the nature of
support for extending governmental aid to particular groups
of citizens. She is interested descriptively in who supports
whom for what reasons. That in itself counts as an important
scholarly contribution. For, as Cook convincingly shows, the
nature of current public opinion research does not permit
one to know with any precision the nature, magnitude, or
basis of American support for social welfare programs.

While the book addresses the nature of American opinion
regarding welfare state choices, the opinions investigated are
those of a cross-section of Chicagoans in the middle 1970s.
The analysis persuades this reader, however, that whatever
problems this sample raises for nationwide extrapolation are
more than compensated for by scholarly precision of data
collection, analysis, and discussion.

And the findings presented are unexpected and thus even
more important. The public, we are shown, does not have so
much a view of welfare in general as views of particular
problems that warrant more or less support. It is, in short, a
discriminating public, itself a finding in the light of the claims
of stereotypes on issues of this sort. Moreover, it is a discerning public. But the public is not one of special groups only
supporting programs they are likely to need and not supporting help for others. Instead, there are broadly shared evalua-
tions of who deserves what help, with little variation across
groups in the distribution of attitudes. This homogeneity
stands in illuminating contrast to the heterogeneity of the

judgments about what conditions and age groups deserve help. Here Cook's findings are startling. Many seemingly obvious claims about American opinion are, on the basis of her data, simply not true. Americans do not, for example, believe their elderly should be ignored, and they do not favor children over the elderly, other things equal. They do take into account considerations of fault in supporting social welfare, but victims of natural disasters are not afforded overwhelming support because of that. To itemize further would be to repeat the important and clearly stated findings of the book itself.

But one further word is warranted. This book is about politics as well as public opinion, but in a special sense. It directs itself to a distorted debate about the nature and future of the American welfare state. If leaders repeat unsubstantiated cliches about public support, all of us suffer from the gap between assumption and actuality. One does not need to believe that public opinion should determine solely the targets of welfare state aid to say that the public's opinion should count importantly in those deliberations. At the moment, those opinions are misunderstood and mistakenly represented. Fay Cook's book should make a major contribution to more enlightened debate about the future American welfare state. By clarifying what the American public believes, she advances the discussion of what the American government can and should do about social welfare amidst fiscal stringency.

Theodore R. Marmor

Chapter 1

PUBLIC SUPPORT FOR WELFARE GROUPS IN A

CONTEXT OF INCREASING SCARCITY AND CONFLICT

According to many commentators, the United States may be entering a period of relative scarcity. Productivity is increasing at a slower rate in this decade than in the two previous ones; the cost of raw materials has risen at a dramatically faster rate than inflation; and the percentage of adults in the work force has decreased, largely because of the increasing numbers of retired persons. These and other pressures—such as the costs of meeting pollution, occupational safety, and health requirements—have led to a slowdown of economic growth in recent years which, if continued, would have widespread social implications. Since the pie of goods and services is not increasing at the rates which held in the 1940s, 1950s, and 1960s, particularly difficult decisions about budget allocations have to be made in times when, as President Carter characterized his 1980 budget, allocations are "austere and lean."

Such austerity and leanness come at a time when the American public appears to be calling for restraint in federal, state, and local government spending as seen, for example, in California's Proposition 13 and similar propositions in other states. For the immediate future at least, public demands for

15

fiscal constraint and a slower-growing pie will have important implications for funding social services for groups of people that are considered needy. The period of increasing social service expenditures is over for the foreseeable future and the pie will not grow as fast as it has in the past few decades to meet growing demands. Instead, the difficult task confronts us of cutting a smaller pie in a context where there is likely to be a heightened sense of competition among the potential service recipients who want to partake of the pie (Gilbert, 1977a and b).

Policy-makers are inevitably confronted with the need to make decisions about the allocation of funds for social services. In a period of relative scarcity, the task is all the more difficult because it is likely to be carried out in a politicized atmosphere where groups with competing interests are vying with each other to protect their share of the pie. On a national level, decisions about how funds get distributed among needy groups are made in Congress, the White House, and the upper echelons of the Department of Health, Education, and Welfare. However, policy-makers in state and local governments are also involved in decisions about allocative priorities. Ultimately, the members of the general public do not make binding choices about resource distributions. However, public opinion on these issues is reflected in the decisions of many officials, even if only at the level of their own estimates of what they think the general public—or particular constituencies within the public—will tolerate in the social welfare arena. To have their decisions implemented, the persons who decide on resource distribution usually have to take into consideration "what the public will countenance" (Gilbert and Specht, 1974; Miller, 1978; Califano, 1978). Program planners too try to understand public preferences for services for welfare groups, for they find it easier to state their case for more tax dollars and to provide effective services if they have adequate legislative and community support (Miller, 1978). Given the role of public preferences,

it would be useful to have a clear, empirical understanding of
the welfare groups the general public most wants to support,
the services it is prepared to countenance for each group, and
the reasons why it differentiates between groups in any way
that it does. An attempt to provide that understanding is the
purpose of this book.

It reports the results of a survey undertaken to learn about
differences in the public's willingness to support social services for a variety of potentially needy groups of people—
hereafter called social welfare groups: the poor elderly, the
physically disabled elderly, poor adults under 65, disabled
adults under 65, poor children, disabled children, and disaster
victims. It probes such questions as these: Which social
groups are considered needy and deserving of help? What
types of social services is the public willing to finance for the
social groups in question? Why is the public willing to support some groups more than other groups? To what extent
do various constituencies within the public agree about support preferences for social groups?

The issue here is not how much weight the public's support preferences should have in decision-making, for there are
many other causal factors that determine decisions. The issue
is that public opinion is considered as *one* input among
others and that currently, as we shall presently attempt to
show, the accuracy and level of differentiation of perceptions
about public opinion are questionable. Furthermore, in periods of scarcity when competition among social welfare
groups may be intensified and when the atmosphere of decision-making may be more politicized, the public opinion
input needs to be based on comparative studies of support
for different welfare groups, not on decision-makers' personal
impressions or social stereotypes about public support or on
the public's answers to global questions about support for
"social welfare" in general.

The purpose of this first chapter is to discuss four major
premises on which our investigation is based. First, tax re-

sources for social services for welfare groups are limited, and, whether we like it or not, a variety of needy groups are potentially in conflict, vying for access to these scarce resources. Second, because we are in a period of stable or contracting budgets, it is likely that competition among groups will grow in the next few years. Third, public preferences play some role—of debatable magnitude, to be sure—in policy-making and program planning in the social service area. And fourth, there is currently no systematic information about differences in public willingness to support a variety of welfare groups.

GROUPS IN COMPETITION FOR SCARCE RESOURCES

Until quite recently, a broad premise underlying governmental policy was the "desirability of unrestrained growth—growth in the economy, in consumer goods and consumerism, in freedom, in size, in power, and finally in government" (Morris, 1979: 2). However, the sense is growing in the United States that unqualified growth is no longer possible due to limitations in physical resources as well as in human tolerance (Samuelson, 1976: 814). Moreover, due to a high inflation rate, balance of trade deficits, and a dramatic slow-down in U.S. productivity, there is not the wealth being created that can be dispersed. The tenth edition of Paul Samuelson's classic text *Economics* contains some revisions that bear testimony to the possibly new "no growth" economic era. Samuelson adds sections on the "new" problem of "scarcity" in a number of areas (e.g., agriculture and energy), and he moves the debates on "limits to growth" to a new stage (1976: ix). In pointing out that "Zero Economic Growth" is a goal "set by concerned people who are alarmed at the exhaustion of the globe's irreplaceable resources and at deterioration of environmental ecological balance," he asks: "How can a modern economy manage—if it should want to—to raise the *quality* of its economic life and forego mere *quantitative* growth?" (1976: 2).

This is a crucial question for policy-makers in the social welfare area. It is becoming a sad fact of policy life that tax resources for welfare groups are limited and that, like it or not, many needy groups are potentially in conflict, vying for access to scarce funds. Of course, a certain amount of conflict exists even when resources are not scarce, but scarcity clearly exacerbates competition. We observe here three sources of conflict: (1) the ceiling on social services funding, (2) the mechanism of Title XX of the Social Security Act, and (3) the traditional categorical approach to giving aid in the United States.

The Ceiling on Social Service Funding

"Social services" refer to those programs designed to help individuals and families cope with a variety of problems of modern life, including emotional distress, insufficient income, lack of education and training, and so forth. They may be seen as "communal provisions" to "promote individual and group well-being and to aid those in difficulty" (Kahn, 1973).[1]

At one time it may have seemed that there would be ever increasing funds for social services. Grants to states for services were seen as an "ever growing" effort by the federal government to help the poor, the sick, and the handicapped (Derthick, 1975: 2). Between 1963 and 1971 federal grants to states for social services under the public assistance titles of the Social Security Act grew more than threefold, from approximately $194 million to $740 million. In 1972 the amount jumped to $1.7 billion. When estimates for 1973 indicated a potential increase to $4.7 billion, Congress enacted a $2.5 billion ceiling on federal expenditures for social services (Derthick, 1975).[2] This limitation on funds is one source of the competition among groups: The funds are fixed whereas the numbers of people in social welfare groups and the needs of these groups are far from fixed.

Title XX

Another source of competition among groups is the structure and design of Title XX of the Social Security Act enacted by Congress in 1974 and implemented in 1975. It established a consolidated program of federal bloc grants to states for social services that replaced most of the categorical grants for social services to the blind, disabled, and aged poor (Title VI grants) and families with dependent children (Title IV-A grants). With these bloc grants come some federal guidelines, but the states are given considerable latitude to design social services tailored to their specific needs.

The problem of heightened competition among potential service recipients arises because Title XX brought with it *no new funds*—there was the same $2.5 billion federal ceiling for social service funding—but brought *new* requirements for public participation in the planning process and *new* and expanded eligibility criteria for entitlement. Under Title XX, public hearings must be held on each state plan for provision of services, and public comment must be taken on the plan for at least 45 days. It is at these hearings that the vying among groups becomes most obvious (Morris, 1979: 125). States are required to use at least 50 percent of their federal funds for services to welfare recipients, which include Aid to Families with Dependent Children, Supplemental Security Income, and Medicaid.[3] What is new about Title XX is that states *may* offer services free of charge to people whose incomes do not exceed 80 percent of the state's median income adjusted for family size, and at reasonable income-related fees to people whose incomes do not exceed 115 percent of the state's median income adjusted for family size. Thus, whereas formerly eligibility was limited to past, current, or potential public assistance recipients, Title XX provides potential admission of a large segment of the nonpoor middle class into the public social services network. To states goes the "unpleasant task of deciding how to distribute limited funds over a wider spectrum of demands" (Morris, 1979: 125). The "inevitable result," according to several experts, is to "heighten competition among potential service recipients" (Gilbert, 1977: 65a and b).

This competition may be seen in public hearings where advocacy groups make their case for services. It is also seen in the publications that advocacy organizations for these groups distribute. For example, the National Council on Aging published "Making Title XX work: a guide for funding social services for older people" (Melemed, 1976). Its purpose is "to provide the information necessary to develop effective state and local level strategies for increasing the availability of services for older persons" (Melemed, 1976: vii). The Hecht Institute for State Child Welfare Planning of the Child Welfare League of America has published similar material to help children's advocates more successfully compete for funds: "Using Title XX to serve children and youth," "Finding federal money for children's services" (Hecht Institute, 1977), and "Child advocates checklist" (Mueller, 1977).

Categorical Aid

A final source of competition among groups is latent and so institutionalized that some may not consider it a way that groups are potentially seen as pitted against each other: the categorical approach to social welfare provision. It serves to define the actors on the policy stage. Rather than giving aid to individuals on the basis of need alone, aid is given on the basis of whether or not the individual fits into a particular category for which aid has been designated. The system of categorical aid was institutionalized in the United States by the Social Security Act of 1935, though the system actually dates back to the Elizabethan Poor Law of 1601. A person is eligible or is not eligible for aid, depending on whether he or she fits into a category (1) of age (for example, an elderly poor person may be eligible for Supplemental Security Income (SSI) but not a poor adult under 65 with the same income); or (2) of disability (for example, a disabled adult under 65 who is poor may be eligible for SSI but not an adult with the same income but no disability); or (3) of income (for example, a child under 18 in a poor family may cause that family to be eligible for Aid to Families with Dependent Children (AFDC), but a family of the same size without a child under 18 with an even lower income may not be eligible for any income maintenance program). People who have lost their home through a declared natural disaster may be eligible for a range of services from the federal government, but people who have suffered an equally disastrous situation due to a fire may be eligible for no such federal help.

The categorical approach to social welfare may be one which welfare experts criticize, but it appears to be fairly well entrenched (Axinn and Levin, 1975; Feagin, 1975). Both federal and state legislatures are reluctant to relinquish the authority inherent in their capacity to authorize and fund categorical programs which have clear visibility (Morris, 1979). As long as we have the categorical approach to aid rather than an approach that is based on need alone, decisions will have to be made about which categorical groups should get what funds. These choices inherently and inevitably pit groups against one another.

INCREASING COMPETITION

Choices about "who gets what" may become more difficult in the future. At the same time that budgets appear to be stable or contracting, the numbers of persons in potentially needy groups are increasing. In 1975, approximately 31 million persons of all ages were classified as disabled. In the age group 18-64, about one in ten was disabled (Berkowitz, 1976: 1). In the age group 65 and over, about one in five was disabled (U.S. General Accounting Office, 1977). As a percentage of the population, the number of disabled has increased and is projected to increase further due to medical technology which keeps alive people who would formerly have died from accidents, disease, or birth defects.

The increase in the percentage of the population who is elderly is dramatic. In 1900, one of every 25 persons (3 million) was 65 or over; in 1975, one of every ten persons (22.4 million) was elderly; and by 2000, it is projected that one of every eight persons (30.6 million) will be 65 or over (National Council on Aging, 1978; McFarland, 1977).

While the *proportion* of people below the official poverty level decreased fairly steadily between 1959 when the data were first collected and 1969, the proportion has not changed markedly since 1969. It has ranged between 11 and 12 percent of the population—between approximately 24 and 25 million people (U.S. Bureau of the Census, 1978).

Not only is the size of each of these groups—which, of course, are not mutually exclusive—large, but each has also grown as an organized interest group which demands services as a right of entitlement. Thus, at a time of limited funds, we have larger numbers and stronger voices making their claims. They are heard in the Title XX public hearings and some have had influence enough to be heard at White House-sponsored national conferences—for example, the White House Conference on Handicapped Individuals, May 1977, and the White House Conference on Aging, 1961 and 1971.

While welfare groups are increasing in numbers and in strength, policy-makers—correctly or not—seem to perceive that the public wants tight budgets and restricted spending in all areas, including the social services. They believe that "Proposition 13 fever" is "sweeping the country" (New York

Times, 1979). This comment refers, of course, to the June 6, 1978, passage in California of Proposition 13, a bill which lowered state and local taxation. It limited realty tax to 1 percent of market value, limited assessment increases to 2 percent annually, and based current property values on assessments as of March 1, 1975. In addition, Proposition 13 required that any state tax increases be approved by a two-thirds vote of the state legislature and that new local taxes be approved by a two-thirds vote of "qualified electors" (U.S. General Accounting Office, 1978). In effect, it promised to cut California's property taxes by more than half—from $12 billion to $5 billion per year—and reduce property tax bills by approximately 57 percent (Blaustein, 1978). The result of tax cuts is lowered funds for social services, according to California social workers polled in a recent survey (Gonzalez and Wellborn, 1979). The executive director of the National Association of Social Workers says it "will undermine the state's services to its poor, elderly, and handicapped" (Alexander, 1979) after state surplus funds have been exhausted.

In other states, similar propositions were introduced and passed. According to some commentators, "politicians elsewhere have declared themselves in possession of a new revelation of public preferences" (Blaustein, 1978: 18).

At the federal level, President Carter presented a tight 1980 budget that perhaps reflected "the Proposition 13 fever." Table 1.1 presents 1978 spending, 1979 estimated and approved spending, and the proposed budget for 1980. For the category "education, training, employment, and social services," it can be seen that no increase—in fact, a slight decrease—is recommended for 1980. This would, of course, be a much more significant decrease if it were adjusted for an anticipated inflation rate of about 9 percent.

The prospect for budget growth in the near future does not appear bright. According to Charles Schultz, Chairman of President Carter's Council of Economic Advisors (CEA, 1979), "the pie is growing less rapidly, and both government

Table 1.1: A Comparison of 1980 Proposed U.S. Budget to 1978 and
            1979 Budgets (Million of Dollars)

Description of Major Functions	1978 Actual	1979 Estimate	1980 Projection
National defense	105,186	114,503	125,830
International affairs	5,922	7,312	8,213
Science, space, and technology	4,742	5,226	5,457
Energy	5,861	8,630	7,878
Natural resources and environment	10,925	11,207	11,456
Agriculture	7,731	6,224	4,269
Commerce and housing credit	3,325	2,968	3,390
Transportation	15,444	17,449	17,609
Education, training, employment, social services	26,463	30,656	30,210
Health	43,676	49,136	53,379
Income security	146,212	158,867	179,120
Veterans' benefits	18,974	20,329	20,461
Administration of justice	3,802	4,351	4,388

Source: U.S. Office of Management and Budget, 1979.

and private demand are going to have to be scaled down accordingly." There are many reasons why the pie is not growing at its old rate, and the most important involve problems that cannot easily be resolved in the next decades.

One reason relates to the growing scarcity of cheap natural resources within the United States. Oil and gas are the most publicized of these increasingly scarce resources. Formerly, they were plentiful and easily available; now, more and more of the national demand is being met from foreign sources at prices far above the earlier ones; and all future projections show that the dependence on foreign fuel imports will increase and that extracting the fuels remaining in the United States will be considerably more expensive than before. It would be wrong to see the growing dependence on overseas raw materials and the increasing difficulty of extracting materials in the United States as being problems only with fossil fuels. Lumber is another much-needed and increasingly difficult-to-obtain resource.

In earlier years, Americans did not have to bear the costs of what economists call "externalities." These are factors—like pollution of the air and water—that are not at first reflected in operating costs of a particular enterprise but eventually become social problems for which the community demands a solution. Such solutions lead to less growth than would have taken place without the action to remedy past and present ills. Occupational health and safety requirements and statistical reporting requirements to various governmental agencies are both additional examples of the expanding call for nonproductive but socially useful endeavors.

It has frequently been noted that productivity in the United States has begun to increase at a slower rate since about 1968. According to data in the Economic Report of the President dated January, 1978, productivity in the private nonfarm business economy increased at a steady annual rate of about 2.6 percent between 1950 and 1968. After 1968, however, the increase dropped to about 1.4 percent and after 1973 it dropped even lower. The slow-down in productivity gains may be associated with another change that has taken place in the past decade. Whereas the United States used to be preeminent in technological innovation, with most new patents being registered in this country, Japan and Western Germany now seem to be adopting the mantle of innovation. Fewer inventions may cause lower productivity gains. But even if they do not, the slower rate of productivity gains, if kept up, will mean that a smaller pie will be available in the future.

Scarcer resources, particularly in fuels, the need to pay the costs of pollution, health and safety requirements, and lower productivity gains may all contribute to the slow-down in growth that we have recently been witnessing in the United States. Since these pressures are not all likely to diminish in the next few decades, their influence will be to keep growth nearer to the 3 percent per annum of the late 1970s rather than the much higher figures of the previous decade. Such restricted growth has to be seen in the context of significant demographic shifts, particularly those relating to the increasing percentage of persons who will be elderly and probably retired. One consequence of having a decreasing percentage of adults gainfully employed in the workforce is that fewer workers will be called upon to help support more elderly persons. And this may happen at a time when those workers are less productive on a per capita basis than we would have predicted in the 1950s or 1960s, when the inflation-adjusted costs of the raw materials they work with are more expensive than formerly, and when a larger percentage of the budget has to be spent on such relatively nonproductive factors as pollution control and compliance with mandated health and safety regulations. All of these factors suggest that, short of exciting new technological innovations, the pie will not be much larger in the next decade than it is today, and that the pie left over for social welfare after defense, industrial development, pollution control, and other needs have been met may even be smaller. A pie that ceases to grow and keep up with inflation may well serve to exacerbate any conflicts of interest that exist between claimant groups in the social welfare domain.

ROLE OF PUBLIC PREFERENCES

The actual role of public opinion in policy formulation is open for debate. According to Owen and Schultze, in the annual Brookings Institution's budget analysis *Setting National Priorities* (1976: 599), "individual senators and representatives depend for survival . . . on satisfying the [geographic] constituencies from which they are elected. . . . The politically safe course for any newcomer to Congress is to attend assiduously to his duties as a delegate . . . he had better never forget who sent him to Washington and who keeps him there." In relation to the social service arena, several commentators concur that public opinion has an important function. Feagin (1975: 65-67) lists public attitudes as one of the "external determinants" which influence the shape and operation of social services. Miller (1978: 48) says, "because of potential electoral consequences, members of Congress frequently represent their constituents' opinions in their voting even though they may personally disagree with them. . . . Public opinion affects the development and delivery of welfare services as well as policy. Lawmakers and social welfare professionals alike view negative public attitudes and the apparent loss of 'credibility' in the welfare system as deterrents to reasoned discussion and action on current and future social needs." These views of the importance of public opinion are not grounded in much empirical research. What has been conducted in this area shows little correlation between congressional perceptions of constituents' attitudes with *actual* constituency opinion, especially for social welfare (Miller and Stokes, 1963).

An example may illustrate a possible gap between policymaker perception and actual public opinion. Against the backdrop of "Proposition 13 fever" with newspaper headlines, news magazines, television, and radio informing us that U.S. citizens will not continue to tolerate high taxes, the *perception* of policy-makers and program planners appears to be that little public support exists for tax financed services for needy groups. Yet, a recent Harris nationwide survey (1978) shows otherwise. People were asked whether they would favor or oppose a decrease in local property taxes if it meant a 35 percent cut in the amount their local government would spend on a variety of services including police protection; fire protection; collecting garbage and trash; educating children in the public schools; the number of teachers in the public schools; maintaining and repairing roads; services in public hospitals and health care; and aid to the elderly, disabled, and poor. In fact, the public was more opposed to a cut in aid to these groups than it was to cuts in any other service. Thus, in contrast to the perceptions, it appears that there *is* support for aid to certain welfare groups—the elderly, disabled, and poor.

The Harris survey did not specify how support is distributed among these welfare groups or for what types of services there is support. In a time when such support is being questioned and when groups must compete for ever more finite resources, it is important to learn how the public differentiates its support among these groups. However, although some commentators speak of the importance of public preferences as one factor in shaping social welfare policy, we actually know very little about public preferences for social programs for the groups who come under the heading "social welfare." Why is this? Three speculations can be offered. First, it may be that policy-makers think they already know about the public's preference for various social welfare groups. This could be from intuition or because many public opinion surveys include a question on support for "social welfare" and survey reports have shown that this support has been decreasing since the 1950s. However, the problem with these surveys is that we do not know to whom respondents are referring when they respond. Is it the elderly who are poor? Or poor adults under 65, or who? Moreover, the possibility exists that *different segments* of the general public have *different referents* when they answer a question about "social welfare." If some people are thinking of poor adults under 65 and others of poor children, it would be difficult to assess whether people differ in their attitudes towards social welfare or merely in their understanding of which welfare groups they are rating. In short, "social welfare" covers too many different groups for policy-makers to understand anything about support for particular welfare groups, about preference orderings among the groups, and about differences in support by different segments of the general public.

Second, policy-makers may not be interested in public support for welfare groups because they believe that public comprehension of welfare issues is simplistic and undifferentiated, making it irrelevant as a source for helping determine welfare policy. For example, the public might not discriminate at all among the different social welfare groups. Or, if they do, they might discriminate in ways that have little relevance to existing policy options, perhaps basing their decisions on global images of groups instead of reflections about the special needs of different groups and the resources available for catering to these needs.

Third, policy-makers may think that consulting the public would be useless because it is simplistic to think of a homogeneous public. Instead, the realities of interest group politics, and the obvious sources of heterogeneity in the American public, have probably accustomed them to thinking of the constituencies within the public, some of which have competing interests, rather than in terms of a general public. Any expectation that the different constituencies might significantly disagree with each other about priorities for welfare groups would cause policy-makers to think survey data to be of little use for developing policies. For example, due to self-interest, low-income groups may be more likely to support services for the poor while disabled people may be more likely to support services for the disabled, and the elderly may be more likely to support services for their own age group.

How valid are these reasons for not consulting the public about their preferences in the social welfare area? Is it, in fact true that members of the public are undiscriminating in their decisions about which social welfare groups to support and in their reasoning buttressing the decisions they do make? Is it true that constituencies within the public are at such cross-purposes in their support preferences as to make any such preferences cancel each other out and thus be irrelevant to the formulation of a general policy that will command widespread public support? In the next section, we will see that earlier studies have not given us sufficient answers to these questions.

DIFFERENCES IN PUBLIC PREFERENCES: WHAT DO WE KNOW?

Most previous studies of public attitudes toward the needy and public support for them have not been relevant to assessing which groups are supported more than others. An answer to this question requires respondents to make comparisons among groups, but such studies are rare. For example, the major studies of attitudes toward the elderly (Shanas, 1962; Harris 1975) were not comparative and did not differentiate among different kinds of elderly persons (e.g., the elderly poor or the elderly disabled) or differentiate support for the elderly from support for other groups. The best-known comparative study involving several social welfare groups is by Carter et. al. (1973), but results from it are hard to interpret because respondents were never asked about their support of different groups for the same services. Instead, they were asked about their support for different groups for different services, thereby confounding attitudes toward particular groups and attitudes toward particular services.

Although comparative studies are rare, nevertheless a variety of claims have been made about public preferences for supporting certain groups. For instance, Butler (1975: 140), in his book *Why Survive? Being Old in America,* says there is little support for the elderly: "Society seems to be saying, 'They're old—they don't need much in the way of services.

Don't waste resources on them.' " On the other hand, Schiltz
(1970: 180) says the elderly enjoy special public sympathy
because they are perceived to be particularly needy and deserving. Carter et al. (1973: 18) claim that "public opinion
reserves its most unstinting compassion for the nation's
young," while Maynes (1974: 3) says that victims of natural
disasters are particularly supported. Berkowitz (1976) points
to the singling out of the disabled for special help. Although
these claims are not explicitly comparative in the sense of
specifying that support for one group is greater than for
another, they nonetheless highlight the need to discover how
public support is in fact differentially distributed across
social groups in need. What follows is an examination of
earlier studies describing support-related attitudes.

Differences in Support-Related Attitudes

To detect differences in support for several social welfare
groups, survey respondents must be asked about all the
groups in the context of the same interview. Only two studies
approximate such a goal. One is an eight-state survey of
9,346 respondents by Carter et al. (1973) who presented
respondents with seventeen social services and asked them to
rank the extent to which each of the services made good use
of public funds. Top priority was given to a service for
children (foster care) and a service for the elderly (nursing
homes for the aged ill). However, the data do not permit us
to draw conclusions about a generalized preference since
another service for the elderly was ranked much lower and
some other services for children were also ranked lower.
Thus, there appeared to be no consistent pattern in the
ranking of services for particular age groups (p. 19), though
the authors concluded: "Clearly, public opinion reserves its
most unstinting compassion for the nation's young. Whatever
is necessary to provide a wholesome environment and adequate opportunities for children is strongly favored (p. 18).

The above generalization was hardly warranted. To learn which groups are favored requires a design with a list of services which *all* the relevant groups need (e.g., medical care or transportation), and then respondents should decide to what extent it would be a good use of public funds for each group to receive the service in question. Merely listing a hodgepodge of services, as Carter et al. did, does not allow us to differentiate between support for the group and for the service in question. Only by holding constant the service and varying the group can we test Carter's generalization that children are particularly favored over other age groups.

In the other study which reported differences in public attitudes toward different welfare services, Williamson (1974c) interviewed a sample of white women in the Boston SMSA during the spring of 1972. Respondents were asked to estimate the stigma they thought recipients felt because they received benefits from 12 existing or proposed welfare programs for the poor: Unemployment Compensation, Social Security, four public assistance programs (General Relief, Aid to Families with Dependent Children, Aid to the Permanently and Totally Disabled, and Old Age Assistance), Public Housing, Head Start, three manpower programs (JOBS, New Careers, Work Incentive Program), guaranteed annual income, and the government as employer of last resort. Williamson arbitrarily assigned Unemployment Compensation a rating of 100 and asked respondents to use this as a baseline for rating the stigma associated with the other programs. Respondents reported that the programs which are clearly for poor adults under 65 (General Relief and Aid to Families with Dependent Children) are the *most* stigmatizing, while a universal program for *all* the elderly who have worked, Social Security (Old Age Insurance), has the least stigma. Also ranked as low in stigma was a program for poor children, Head Start. In between the two extremes were Aid to the Permanently and Totally Disabled (with a median stigma ranking of 75) and Old Age Assistance (median of 50).[4] Thus, the order from least to most stigma seems to be (1) the elderly in general, (2) poor children, (3) elderly poor people, (4) physically disabled, and (5) poor adults under 65. Though this study does tell us something about differences in public perceptions of several welfare programs, it has no clear implications for which programs the respondents would be willing to support. This is because no evidence is reported which relates stigma to the willingness to support social programs.

It should be clear by now that neither of these studies was well designed for answering questions about differences in support for particular welfare groups. From the first study we receive (contrary to what the authors say) almost *no* information on which *groups* are favored because the groups are also confounded with services. From the second, we learn which programs respondents think are most stigmatizing to the recipients, but we do not know how respondents would *support* such programs.

Despite the absence of empirical knowledge, we often hear speculations about the relative priorities among social welfare groups. For example, in an introductory text on social work and social welfare, authors Brieland et al. (1975: 32-33) present a "speculative ordering" of which public programs for groups have greater public acceptance. At the top of the hierarchy they place services for physically disabled adults and for disabled children. Next comes child welfare services for poor children. At the bottom of their public acceptance hierarchy are public assistance for the poor and correctional services for offenders. The implicit assumption behind this ordering is that there exists a *generalized preference* for certain groups and that this general ordering applies to preferences regardless of the *particular* service in question. This assumption is tested in the study presented here.

Support for Social Welfare in General

In many polls of political and social attitudes a question has been asked about support for social welfare expenditures in general. Much of our understanding of public support for social welfare groups has come from this single question. Obviously, responses to such a question can provide only a very gross and indirect estimate of how much the public would support individual social welfare groups. Nevertheless, the responses need to be considered since they represent, for some researchers and policy-makers, the "general wisdom."

Schiltz (1970) analyzed dozens of public opinion surveys conducted from 1935 to 1965 by Gallup Poll, Elmo Roper (chiefly for *Fortune Magazine*), the National Opinion Research Center (NORC), and the Survey Research Center at the University of Michigan. In one section of his study, Schiltz extracted and organized answers to questions on 15 surveys between 1935 and 1964 which asked respondents about their support for an increase or decrease in welfare expenditures. As Schiltz points out himself, there are many limitations to such a survey of surveys. A major problem is that only a single question about welfare support is asked, and this is phrased differently from survey to survey. Thus, the single question restricts the information yield (see Schiltz, 1970: 181-84), and any differences in result across time may reflect changes in specific wording rather than changes in public attitudes. With these caveats in mind, it should be noted that Schiltz's data reveal a rise in the public's preference for increased government expenditures for welfare from 1948 to 1961, then a sharp drop. In 1948, 45 percent of the population wanted an increase while 60 percent did in 1961. However, in the early 1960s, support began to drop until it reached 18 percent by 1964.

More recent data have been reported by Katona (1974, 1975) and Curtin and Cowan (1975) who conducted secondary analyses of several Survey Research Center nationwide surveys in which questions about public attitudes toward government programs were asked. One question was about public welfare, and respondents were asked whether they felt more, less, or the same amount should be spent for federal welfare programs. The percentage of respondents wanting heavier spending for education, medical care, low-income housing, and highway construction showed virtually no change from 1961 to 1973. However, support for both welfare and defense expenditures eroded in the sixties and early seventies. By 1973, the proportion of respondents favoring increased federal spending for welfare stood at 28 percent whereas in 1969 it had been 36 percent and in 1961 60 percent (Curtin and Cowan, 1975: 58).

Taylor (1976) has conducted the most recent time series study, examining five nationwide surveys conducted in 1950, 1961, 1973, 1974, and 1975. He also found a similar decrease in welfare support. The proportion favoring increased spending in 1950 was 43.9 percent; in 1961, 40.2 percent; in 1971, 19.9 percent; in 1973, 20.7 percent; in 1974, 23.1 percent; and in 1975, 24.7 percent (Taylor, 1975: 134).

Though it is often assumed that these surveys correctly estimate the proportion who support tax-financed social services for *all* welfare groups, this assumption is doubtful. Responses to a general question about social welfare provide no information about the respondent's referent group, i.e., whether the respondent is thinking about poor children, the physically disabled, the elderly poor, or several groups at once. Unless the respondent is allowed to differentiate among welfare groups, policy-makers get a less than accurate understanding of public willingness to support welfare. Yet their estimate of public willingness to support social services probably depends more on responses to general questions about public welfare than to any other sort of social science information.

Earlier Studies Seeking to "Explain" Support-Related Attitudes

Though it would be useful merely to be able to describe public preferences in the support of our seven welfare groups, it would be even more useful to explain such preferences. By "explain" we understand the elicitation of the cognitive bases for offering support. Explanatory constructs might therefore take the form: "We particularly prefer to give tax monies to the disabled elderly for nutrition services *because they are disabled through no fault of their own.*" In this particular hypothetical example, the explanatory construct would be "not responsible for plight."

Explanatory concepts are useful because they provide a basis for predicting the conditions under which a particular relationship holds, thereby extending generalizability. Thus, even if the research dealt with only seven groups, we could all the more confidently predict findings for an eighth or ninth or tenth group. For example, suppose we find that those groups seem as not responsible for their plight receive more support than those seen as responsible for their condition. Then we would expect that if we added another group who was shown as not responsible for its plight, support for it would be high also.

Since no previous surveys asked the same respondents questions about a number of social welfare groups, it is obviously not possible to review past studies on reasons for any differences or similarities in support. However, clues from various sources can help us compile a list of possible explanatory constructs. One source is the social-psychological literature on "helping behavior" which we are prepared to assume is a cognate of "support." A second is survey data on correlates of support for "social welfare." Third, speculation by knowledgeable scholars may be useful. The following sections represent some gleanings from these sources.

CHARACTERISTICS OF THE PERSONS TO BE SUPPORTED

Need. Several experimental studies have been conducted of psychological determinants of "helping behavior." Many of these studies found that persons in need were helped more than persons with less need (e.g., Berkowitz and Conner, 1966; for a summary, see Krebs, 1970: 277). Moreover, greater intensity of a person's need seems to result in greater probability of a potential helper's responsiveness (Schwartz, 1975). Unfortunately, most of the relevant studies took place in laboratory settings or, if they took place in the field, involved short experimental manipulations of short-lasting needs. They were therefore far removed from real life conditions where need can be caused by poverty, disability, and disasters which we are studying here.

Survey research has not provided us with any clear-cut causal findings about the psychological causes of support. However, some survey evidence points toward perception of need as an important element in determining support for welfare groups. Mueller (1963) found that 60 percent of the respondents in a nationwide survey favored government spending on "help for needy people," whereas in the same year the American Institute for Public Opinion found that a low 35 percent in October and an even lower 27 percent in November favored spending more money on "welfare programs." A strong possibility exists that the difference in support was due to the difference in the designations "needy people" and "welfare programs."

Locus of responsibility for need. Although apparent need (or dependency) seems to elicit helping, laboratory research in the field of social psychology indicates that supportive behavior may not follow invariably from perceptions of need. Rather, such a response may depend upon a more complex evaluative process in which various types of need are distinguished. Shopler and Matthews (1965), Horowitz (1968), and Berkowitz (1966) found that need caused by external forces beyond the victim's control elicited more help than need which arose because of the victim's own behavior. Externally caused need was also seen as more legitimate than self-caused need.

Considerable speculation links the notion of a welfare group's responsibility for its plight to the willingness of the public to help the group. For example, Berkowitz (1976: 2) believes that the physically disabled are "singled out" for help because "society feels a special obligation to a class of unfortunates *who cannot be held responsible for their condition.*" He further speculates, "disability is recognized as legitimate and met with sympathetic understanding on the part of the public insofar as the cause of disability and the consequent need for benefits are thought to be *beyond the control of the individual.*" Feagin (1975: 92) presents an argument that ties together the public's unwillingness to support much assistance to the poor to the public's belief that "those who are economically unsuccessful, the poor, *must bear the responsibility themselves.*" (Emphases in this paragraph are ours.) The social psychological research as well as speculations such as those cited above were important elements in our decision to add "locus of responsibility for plight" to the list of possible explanatory constructs worth incorporating into our measurement and analysis framework.

Gratefulness. How grateful a social welfare group is seen to be may influence a person's decision to give help. The sociological and social-psychological literature on "the reciprocity norm" (Gouldner, 1960) demonstrates that people feel social relationships to be more stable and satisfactory if there is reciprocity—i.e., "you did something for me so I do something for you." However, some people do not have the resources to reciprocate. Thus, we have developed mechanisms of symbolic reciprocation from the smile of thanks to the public expression of gratefulness. But when power relationships are unequal and the relatively disadvantaged party can only respond with gratefulness to concrete acts of aid, this can easily degenerate into a situation where people of lower power resent the help they are given, as may be the case with welfare workers and welfare recipients or developed and developing nations.

The point to be noted is that persons with high power who help others find relationships more satisfying if the persons they help show gratitude. However, the task in this study is to explain the support of the majority who are in a position to give support rather than the minority who are only in a position to accept it. It could be speculated that so much of the supposed opposition to helping the poor is due to the public's perception that the poor are not grateful for the help they receive but instead are resentful. On the other hand, the portrayal of disaster victims in some media reports is replete with expressions of gratitude and thanks to individuals who helped the victims, whether the helpers were public officials paid to give aid or neighbors and strangers who volunteered to help. All of this leads to the hypothesis that social groups which respond gratefully for help may be assigned higher priorities for social service funds allocated from the welfare budget.

Deservingness. How deserving a group is perceived to be may also influence a person's decision to give help. "Deservingness" has been a criterion for receiving state-funded aid since the Elizabethan Poor Law of 1601. This statute established programs for the destitute, depending upon age and ability to work. The able-bodied "sturdy beggar" was treated as "undeserving" and was subjected to a work test, while the aged and severely disabled were viewed as "deserving" and exempted from work. In the opinion of many authors of social welfare texts (Coll, 1969; Axinn and Levin, 1975; Bremner, 1956; Woodroofe, 1962), the dichotomy between "the deserving" and "the undeserving" has stuck, and society is willing to give aid to those groups it considers deserving— the same groups that were considered deserving in 1601—the aged and severely disabled.

Several surveys which were conducted to understand attitudes toward the poor uncovered quite negative attitudes (Feagin, 1975; Goodwin, 1972; Alston and Dean, 1972;

Lauer, 1971; Rytina et al., 1970; Williamson, 1974a, b, c). These studies show that "the poor" are often still seen to be undeserving. Although social welfare commentators have speculated that there is a link between the perception of deservingness and willingness to give support for a variety of social welfare groups, this linkage has not been empirically demonstrated. That is one of the aims of this study.

Pleasantness. Another influence on a person's decision to give help may be his perception of how "pleasant" a welfare group is. According to Berkowitz (1975: 179), people are attractive to others because they have the physical, psychological, and social qualities that others find pleasant. Furthermore, "them's that has (the characteristics that make them attractive) gets (popularity from a great many different persons)." Experimental social-psychological research on helping behavior suggests that "them that has" attractiveness and/or pleasantness may also be helped more (Bryan and Test, 1967; Deaux, 1976). All things being equal, people we like and find attractive and pleasant seem to get more help. These findings come from experimental research in quite contrived situations. Our task is to understand whether people use such attributes when they have to make decisions about supporting social welfare groups.

PSYCHOLOGICAL CHARACTERISTICS OF RESPONDENTS

Self-Interest. People's level of self-interest may be one determinant of their willingness to support social welfare groups. By "self-interest" we mean simply that people will support something if it could have direct value for themselves. In a 1961 nationwide probability survey of public attitudes toward fiscal programs, Mueller (1963) found that twice as many "repeatedly unemployed" people favored larger unemployment insurance benefits than did those "never unemployed."

Mueller also found that low-income people favored more spending on programs of direct benefit to lower-income groups—hospital and medical care, public works, and help for needy people—than did upper-income people. It would have been helpful if Mueller could have probed the respondents in greater depth about why they favored these particular programs; for example, did they see the programs as benefiting themselves? Or because they were low income, did they simply understand the service needs of poor people and thus support programs for them? Her conclusion about "direct personal benefit" was that it offered only a partial explanation of attitudes toward fiscal programs.

More recent analyses of survey data have led to contradictory findings about whether self-interest determines support. Analyzing the *same data,* Katona (1975) and Curtin and Cowan (1975) reached opposite conclusions. Katona argued that the data did *not* support the notion that preferences for spending programs depend on self-interest, while Curtin and Cowan said the data did. Clearly, more work must be done in this area before the issue can be settled.

Perhaps one of the first things that must be done is to define more clearly the conditions of self-interest under which a person might be motivated to give more help to a particular social welfare group. Very simply, they might be: (1) the respondent *belongs* to the particular welfare group; (2) the respondent thinks it highly likely that he or she might *become* a member of the welfare group; (3) the respondent *knows* a relative or a close friend who is in the welfare group. Each of these three conditions will be explored as possible self-interest reasons for some groups receiving more support than others.

Belief in a just world. People's personal view of the world may be another determinant of their willingness to support social welfare groups. Lerner (1965, 1970) has postulated that many believe that the world is a place where people deserve their fates, where good people are rewarded and bad people punished. Others, according to him, believe that the world is unjust, that success and failure are often random events, and that people do not necessarily deserve their fates. Of course, one does not have to hold such a belief in extreme fashion. Rather, belief in a just world has been considered a continuum ranging from a very strong belief, through to ambivalence, through to believing that injustice prevails.

There is growing evidence from laboratory research of the utility of the construct "belief in a just world." For instance, Lerner (1965) found that observers persuaded themselves that a worker rewarded by chance had performed better than a partner who was deprived by chance. Walster (1966) found that the more serious the outcome of a person's acts, the more an observer will want to find the person responsible for the outcome. Lerner and Simmons (1966) found that observers described an innocent victim as less attractive when they thought her suffering would continue than (a) if they thought her suffering had ended; or (b) if they saw her apparently unaffected after the event; or (c) if they had received confirmation that she would be rewarded. Such experiments suggest that individuals "arrange their cognitions so as to maintain the belief that people get what they deserve or, conversely, deserve what they get" (Lerner and Simmons, 1966: 204; see also Rubin and Peplau, 1973).

DEFINING THE QUESTIONS: WHAT DO WE WANT TO KNOW?

Any examination of differences in public support for social welfare groups must carefully define and operationalize "support" and have a rationale for selecting the groups to be compared.

Support can simply be thought of in terms of positive feelings, and it could be measured by having respondents rank the chosen welfare groups in order from least to most favored. Or, support can be conceptualized as willingness to *do* something to ameliorate the condition of a particular group. In the modern state where, for the most part, tax-supported federal aid to needy persons has replaced individual charity and church-related tithes, "willingness to do something" might be willingness to pay higher taxes to finance services for a group; it might be willingness to write a letter to someone in government advocating more services; it might be willingness to attend a local public meeting to bring about such services; or it might be the distribution of more funds to one group than another. In this book we shall use "support" in the sense of a reported willingness to do something, to advocate services for a particular group or to have taxes raised to help them. Considerable evidence suggests that such "behavioroid" measures are better predictors of behavior than more affect- or cognition-laden measures of attitude, although behavioroid measures do not perfectly predict behavior (cf., Fishbein and Ajzen, 1975).

The social welfare groups selected for study include three subgroups of those who are poor:

    (1) poor children,
    (2) poor adults under 65,
    (3) poor elderly persons;

three subgroups of the physically disabled:

    (4) physically disabled children,
    (5) physically disabled adults under 65,
    (6) physically disabled elderly persons;

and persons of any age who are victims of a natural disaster

    (7) disaster victims.

One rationale for the selection of these particular groups is that they are obviously needy groups for whom society has already accepted *some* degree of responsibility for the provision of social welfare services. The case can be made that these groups receive most of the federal funds in the social welfare arena; and that being the principal recipients of social welfare funds, they are already in competition. For reasons of demography and medical progress, we might expect the conflict to exacerbate as the numbers of potential recipients increase while the pool of resources fails to increase at close to the same rate.

A second rationale for selecting these groups is to allow an examination of the effect on public willingness to give help of (1) the age of the group (children, adults under 65, elderly); (2) the condition of the group (poverty, disability, disaster); and (3) the joint effect of age and poverty/disability. Therefore, we are not limited to conclusions about global categories such as "the elderly" within which there are significant sources of variability that might well affect to whom the public thinks aid for the elderly should be distributed. For instance, is support for the elderly who are disabled distributed differently from support for aid for the elderly who are poor? If so, which services are preferred for each group? And is the preference for, say, the disabled over the poor among the elderly age group also found when ratings are made for children? By means of finer-grained analysis within the principal categories that determine where much (but not all) current aid is distributed, we hope to explore significant sources of support that may often be overlooked. In addition, we can test whether the public makes discernments between different kinds of elderly adults and younger adults as well as children.

Choosing the social welfare groups to study was not an easy task, and the ones we selected are not exhaustive, though we think they are the principal ones. One of the groups may be seen as a somewhat unusual choice for inclusion—victims of natural disasters. This is a group who experiences needs for social services when disaster strikes just as when poverty or disability occurs, and it is a group on which the federal government has expended more tax supported funds in the last few years than previously (White and Haas, 1975). One rationale for including this group was that we thought it would be useful in increasing the variability among the groups on some of the potential explanatory constructs. For example, we anticipate that most persons think disaster victims not at all responsible for their fate. Will this perception be related to more support for them than for other groups?

The Research Questions

The survey described here has two sections: a descriptive section and an explanatory section. The descriptive section attempts to describe patterns of support, while the explanatory section attempts to explain these patterns. Since descriptive surveys are superior in answering questions about naturally occurring associations and controlled experiments are superior in answering questions about causation, the study reported here combines both features of research design.

The descriptive section of the survey has three major purposes. One is to discover which of the seven welfare groups are most supported by the general public when it comes to allocating support. Earlier in the chapter, we discussed the claims that children (Carter et al., 1973), disaster victims (Maynes, 1974), the physically disabled (Berkowitz, 1976), or the elderly (Schiltz, 1970) are particularly supported or that the elderly are not supported (Butler, 1975). However, prior research has not been able to describe actual differences in public preferences because none has given survey respondents the opportunity to differentiate among groups on the same question in the context of the same interview. Respondents were given that opportunity in the research described here. The data gathered should provide us with information about the role of the welfare group's poverty, disability, and age in determining support given.

The second purpose of the descriptive part of the survey is to examine possible differences in patterns of support for social welfare groups across nutrition, income, education, and transporation services. It is important to discover the extent to which the general public is discerning in the support it offers. The possibility exists that the public has stereotypes about each group which predispose it to support some groups more than others, *irrespective of the service* for which support is asked. If the public is not very discerning and fails to relate support to each group's particular needs, then the case is weakened for using public opinion as one of the inputs deciding allocative priorities. If, on the other hand, the public is more discerning and supports some groups for some services but other groups for other services, then we think that this would at the very least increase the weight of evidence which suggests that it would be worthwhile considering public opinion when deciding on priorities for support.

The third purpose of the descriptive part of the survey is to examine the way in which different subgroups within the public differentiate among the seven welfare groups. Up to this point, we have discussed "public opinion" as though it were a single, homogeneous voice. But we know that on a wide range of issues such homogeneity is an illusion. We know this from past opinion research on a host of topics, from basic notions in political science about interest groups and their support of priorities that favor their welfare, and from elementary notions in marketing about segments of the general public with different needs, tastes, and preferences. Seen from the context of interest group politics, we would expect some groups in the general public consistently to prefer to support social welfare groups to which they do or might belong. From the concept of market segmentation and experiential knowledge of the heterogeneity of preferences and values within the United States, we might expect different sections of the public consistently to support certain groups more than other groups. If these speculations are correct, we would expect to find considerable variability in the groups that are preferred over others for any particular service. Obviously, if there is this variability, it makes the use of public opinion data all the more problematic when difficult decisions have to be made about resource allocations for welfare groups. On the other hand, if there is little variability and the public is homogeneous in its preferences, this implies that anyone using public opinion data as one of the criteria for reaching decisions would be using data that indicate considerable popular support for the action suggested by the data. In the study reported here, we divided the public into 16 groups, formed by factorially combining two race groups (black and white), three income groups (high, moderate, and low), two age groups (under 50, and over 50), and two sex groups. These variables were all chosen because of their traditional use in survey research, but also because the first three of them could help probe the extent to which support for the poor and disabled of various age groups is linked to self-interest.

The purpose of the explanatory section of the survey is to probe why some groups are supported more than others. It is extremely useful to discover the forces that mediate support. The elucidation of explanatory constructs can help planners develop perspectives (1) which may help them *reduce* the link between a given group and reasons for not supporting it or (2) which may help them *forge* a link between the group and reasons for supporting it that were not previously seen as linked to the group. For example, if we learn that more support goes to people who have a chronic condition than those who have an acute condition, and if we want to gain support for the chronically disabled, then we know that the chronicity of the disability must be stressed. Or we may learn that little support goes to poor people if they have caused their own poverty; then, in getting public backing for services for a group of poor adults under 65, it would be useful if factors other than individual ones could be shown to have caused the poverty.

Explanatory constructs will be explored through traditional survey questions as well as through an experiment embedded in the survey. Experiments are superior for testing causal links, while surveys are more useful for answering descriptive questions. As will be elaborated in detail in Chapter 2, we combine the two approaches in order to achieve the strength of each research approach for description and explanation.

A list of potential explanatory constructs resulted from a review of literature on helping behavior, survey literature, and speculations of knowledgeable scholars. Some explanatory constructs to be examined have to do with the welfare groups: responsibility for plight, need, gratefulness, pleasantness, and deservingness. Others have to do with the respondents: level of belief in a just world and whether they belong to a particular welfare group or think they could belong or have relatives or close friends who are in the welfare group.

SUMMARY

Evidence indicates that in the past few years some tax-based social welfare services have not been growing as fast as inflation and the number of new persons in need. Evidence also suggests that many members of the public are unwilling to pay higher taxes and that many politicians are heeding their complaints. For these reasons, and for many more structural economic reasons, it is likely that social welfare budgets will not noticeably increase in the immediate future.

A likely consequence of stable or decreasing budgets and of growing numbers of persons in need or claiming need is that competition will be exacerbated among needy groups. Most of this competition will be found in the arena of power politics. But it is likely, even in that arena, that some cognizance will be taken of public opinion about the social welfare groups that are most likely to be supported for particular services. Since little is known at present about public support for services, the purpose of this book is to probe five questions. The first two stress describing who is given help. They are:

(1) Which social welfare groups does the public most prefer to support for a variety of tax-based social services?

(2) To what extent is this support made contingent on the particular services for which funds are required?

To answer these questions we used four services (nutrition, transportation, education, and income guarantees), and seven welfare groups (the elderly poor, the elderly disabled, poor adults under 65, disabled adults under 65, poor children, disabled children, victims of natural disasters).

The third question emphasizes segments of the general public who are called upon to give support:

(3) To what extent is the general public homogeneous in the way it allocates support to the social welfare groups and services we examined?

The fourth question is explanatory rather than descriptive:

(4) Why are there the differences in support for social welfare groups that appear in the descriptive part of the study?

No answer to these four questions would be complete without a discussion of:

(5) What are the theoretical and policy implications of any findings about which groups are preferred for which service by which segments of the general public and for which reasons?

The next chapters address these issues. Chapter 2 explains the research design. Chapter 3 discusses the first two questions listed above. Chapter 4 examines the third question, and Chapter 5 addresses the fourth question. The sixth chapter explores the policy and theoretical implications of the findings.

NOTES

1. The Department of Health, Education, and Welfare has defined social services as having one or more of the following goals: (1) achieving or maintaining economic self-support; (2) achieving or maintaining self-sufficiency; (3) preventing or remedying neglect, abuse, or exploitation of children and adults unable to protect their own interests, or preserving, rehabilitating or reuniting families; (4) preventing or reducing inappropriate institutional care by providing for community-based or home-based care or other forms of less intensive care; (5) securing institutional care when other forms of care are not appropriate.

2. These grants are not the only source of funding for social services. Services to groups are also provided through other sources: the Department of Agriculture, the Economic Opportunity Act of 1964, the Demonstration Cities and Metropolitan Development Act of 1966, and Title IV-B of the Social Security Act.

3. The mandated service requirements are: (1) At least one service must be directed at one of the goals in each of Title XX's five goal categories; (2) at least three types of service must be selected by the state to serve recipients of SSI; (3) family planning services must be available to AFDC recipients who request them.

4. Aid to the Permanently and Totally Disabled, Old Age Assistance, and Aid to the Blind were incorporated into one federal program, Supplemental Security Income (SSI) in 1974.

Chapter 2

THE RESEARCH DESIGN

This chapter presents the methods that were used to answer the research questions outlined in Chapter 1. The chapter is in four sections. First, we outline the general approach taken to answering the descriptive and explanatory questions, stressing the need for (1) traditional survey methodology for addressing descriptive concerns and (2) traditional experimental methods for addressing explanatory concerns that involve hypotheses about causal relationships. Second, we describe the sample and the field procedures used to collect the data. Third, we detail the traditional survey methods that were used to answer primarily the descriptive research questions. Finally, we describe the experiment that was developed primarily to probe why some welfare groups might receive more tax-based support than others.

MEETING THE DESCRIPTIVE AND
EXPLANATORY GOALS

Opinion surveys are the traditional social science vehicles for answering descriptive questions about such matters as the groups most supported for social services and the extent to which support preferences are shared by different segments of the public. Surveys achieve their goals by selecting representative (or at least, heterogeneous) samples of respondents who respond to carefully worded items in carefully implemented interviews that tap into their beliefs. Surveys have had a very successful history in answering descriptive questions about preferences among a set of alternatives.

Surveys are also used to examine causal questions, following a process that has several steps. First, the possible explanatory constructs are listed and explicated. At this stage, some may be rejected on grounds of being implausible, leaving only a subset for further study. The constructs are then incorporated into a causal model with specified links between presumed cause and effect variables. The model serves as a guide for operationalizing the constructs of interest, and several measures of each construct are designed and validated. The data are then collected and examined. Variables that do not correlate with the outcome variable—in this case, differences in support for welfare groups—are considered not to be adequate explanations because explanatory constructs should at least correlate with what they are supposed to explain. Variables that do correlate with the outcome variable cannot necessarily be considered as explanatory. They only achieve this status once the researcher rules out alternative interpretations of the correlation between the outcome variable and the potential explanatory variable of interest. Usually, some form of regression analysis is used to examine the relationship of the potential explanatory variable and the outcome variable, for regression is supposed to hold constant the influence of one or more possible alternative interpretations.

This kind of method, with its stress on control through passive measurement, and a single wave of measurement, is generally not useful in testing causal propositions when the extant theory in a particular substantive area is weak, as is the case with support for welfare groups (Duncan, 1975;

Heise, 1975; Cook and Campbell, 1976). There are many reasons for this weakness of surveys, the major ones being: ambiguity about the direction of causal inference, selection artifacts masquerading as treatment effects, and variables with higher reliability spuriously emerging as causes because high reliability leads to higher correlations and higher standardized regression coefficients.

Randomized experiments are more suitable in testing causal hypotheses. The assignment process makes the order of temporal precedence clear, unconfounds treatment and selection effects, and does away with the need to base causal inference on the competition between presumed "independent" variables that have been fallibly measured, possibly with differential reliability.

In the present study, we are trying to understand *why* different welfare groups receive different levels of support, and we use both a survey and an experiment to examine this issue. Though this question is explanatory, we could not answer it solely on the basis of an experiment since experiments like the one to be described here answer a special contingency question about causal relationships that is of low external validity. Let us explain this. When respondents are presented with hypothetical vignette characters whose attributes have been deliberately tailored by the researcher to reflect possible causes of support, the responses permit us to learn the different consequences of each attribute, whether it be "level of need" or "responsibility for plight." But the responses do not permit us to learn whether respondents *spontaneously* perceive welfare groups as differing on the very attributes that the researcher builds into the vignettes. Stated differently, the simulation experiment informs us about factors that *can* cause differences in support for welfare groups if individuals *do* associate these factors with the groups, but it does not inform us whether individuals do *in fact* associate these factors with groups in the "real world." The survey with its direct probing of the characteristics attributed to various welfare groups—e.g., level of need, whether their plight is self-caused or not—has a greater descriptive fidelity than the experiment. Consequently, an experiment does allow us to assess the attributes that are spontaneously associated with groups. Unfortunately, the survey does not allow us to test very well whether these attributes are causally related to differences in the willingness to support welfare groups—a task at which the experimental simulation is better.

The larger task is to weld the greater power of the randomized experiment for making causal inferences with the greater descriptive fidelity of the measurement plan in the survey. In the present study, we attempt to test how similar variables were related to support in both a survey and an experiment. Our hope is to discover that the most powerful correlates of support in the survey are also the strongest causes of support in the experiment. If they are, inference-making will be relatively easy and based on the unique and complementing strengths of each method. For the experiment, with its deliberate manipulations by the researcher, the strength is internal validity and a major weakness is external validity; while for the survey, with its passive measurement and correlational nature, the strength is external validity and the relative weakness internal validity. The greater external validity achieved will allow us to have more confidence in generalizing our findings to constituencies within the survey population at large, while the greater internal validity will allow us to have greater confidence in the variables that might explain any differences in support.

There is another advantage to the use of a traditional survey framework to examine causal issues via both the passive measurement of potential explanatory variables and the active experimental manipulation of some of these variables. This is that some of the descriptive questions we have already outlined can be addressed a second time. We can see from examining the vignette data which kinds of welfare groups are helped more than others; and we can assess how homogeneous the general public is in the patterning of its support for the different groups.

SAMPLE

The universe sampled in this study was the total noninstitutionalized population of Chicago, Illinois, 21 years of age and older. The sample itself was derived from a random sampling first of census tracts and then of blocks within tracts. At the block level, quota sampling was used to obtain equal numbers of Black and white persons belonging to pre-ordained income, sex, and age groups. For each race, 50 percent are male and 50 percent are female. Half of the men and women are under 50 and half are over 50. Finally, each of the age, sex, and race groups is equally stratified into high-, middle-, and low-income groups. The result is a sample that is fully balanced with 16 respondents for every combination of age, race, sex, and income, a total of 384 respondents.

Table 2.1: Sampling Design[a]

				Income	
Race	Sex	Age	Low	Medium	High
Black	Male	Young			
Black	Male	Old			
Black	Female	Young			
Black	Female	Old			
White	Male	Young			
White	Male	Old			
White	Female	Young			
White	Female	Old			

a. Total of 24 demographic cells with 16 respondents in each cell (24 x 16 = 384 respondents).

The design was implemented by using the 1970 U.S. Bureau of the Census statistics to divide Chicago census tracts into predominantly black and predominantly white tracts. Both sets of tracts were then stratified by high, middle, and low total reported household income. In the United States, the median income of whites is significantly higher than that of blacks, and this is true in Chicago as well. For example, in Chicago the highest median census tract income of blacks in 1970 was $19,558 and the lowest was $3,827. For whites, the corresponding figures were $26,123 and $6,750. Because of this income difference, it was decided that black and white census tracts had to be stratified differently, with blacks having lower income in each income stratum than whites.[1] On the basis of 1970 census data, the high, middle, and low income ranges for census tract selections were as follows:

White	Black
$17,291 to $26,123	$12,175 to $19,558
$12,525 to $12,991	$ 7,843 to $ 9,705
$ 6,750 to $ 8,666	$ 3,827 to $ 6,890

After all the Chicago tracts had been stratified, a sample was randomly selected within each race and income stratum. Blocks were then randomly selected within each tract. Interviews were conducted at the block level, with no more than five respondents being interviewed on each block. Strict quota sampling was used at this last stage of the sampling design in order to obtain sex and age quotas of predetermined size. The decision to use quota sampling was made because the cost of quota sampling is substantially less than the cost of interviewing a full probability sample of the same size. There is, of course, a higher chance of sampling biases with quota sampling, mainly due to the systematic biases associated with the respondent being or not being at home when the interviewing is to take place. To reduce this bias, the interviewers were given instructions to canvass and interview only after 4:30 P.M. on weekdays or during the weekend or holidays.

Initially, it was believed that stratification by census tract would be sufficient to obtain the required income quotas. However, after approximately 50 interviews, it was discovered that family income was so variable within tracts that it was difficult to obtain the required quotas within each of the preordained income tracts. Thus for the remainder of the study, repsondents in all tracts were screened for income before the interview was administered, and assignment to income quotas took place irrespective of the average income level of the tract. The screening question in white households was: "My assignment is to interview households where the head of the household and spouse earn (*whatever the interviewer's quota requirement is*—(a) $20,000 or more a year, (b) between $10,000 and $20,000 a year, (c) $10,000 or less a year). Does the head of this household and spouse have a combined income of $ . . . a year?" The same question was asked in black households except that the income cutoff points were different than for whites: over $15,000 per year, between $8,000 and $15,000, and under $8,000.

The interviews were conducted by interviewers from the Institute for Social Action (ISA), Chicago, and the National Opinion Research Center (NORC), Chicago. The interviewers all had at least two years experience in professional interviewing and attended a training session to administer the particular questionnaire for this survey. The field period ran from January 20, 1976, to June 14, 1976. A 20 percent validation check on all interviews was conducted; that is, 20 percent of all respondents were called and asked a series of questions to validate the fact that the interview took place. The final validation checks in June revealed no problems with any interviews.

THE DESCRIPTIVE SECTION OF THE SURVEY

Part of the survey was designed to answer questions that were principally descriptive. These questions focused on who gave more support to particular welfare groups and on respondents' perceptions of each group along a series of dimensions that might explain why some groups received more help than others. A multiple measurement framework was employed, so that several measures were obtained of each of the constructs most crucial for meeting our research objectives.

Measures of Support

"Support" for a social welfare group may be conceptualized in several different ways. It can be simply thought of as *favoring* a particular group. A respondent could rank the seven groups in the order from least to most favored, and "favor" could be thought of in terms of the degree to which a respondent had positive feelings about a group. Support can alternatively be conceptualized as willingness to do something to ameliorate the condition of a particular group. In the present study, "support" is conceptualized in this second sense—as willingness to do something, to advocate services for a particular group. The reason for this is that we were primarily interested in behavioral support, and though resources did not permit a direct study of overt supportive behavior, considerable past literature on the relationship of attitudes to behavior suggests that "behavioroid" measures predict overt behavior better than attitudinal items that have no clear relationship to specific behaviors (Fishbein and Ajzen, 1975). We will now describe these behavioroid measures.

The money distribution measure of support. One support measure we used was based on a simulated distribution of government resources. Respondents were asked to assume roles as policy-makers and to distribute money to a series of services for the seven welfare groups. The services were nutrition, transportation, education, and income. Taking each service separately, the interviewer briefly explained to the respondent how that service—say, transportation—could be used by each welfare group. Then he or she asked the respondent to distribute $100,000 in simulated money among the seven groups for transportation services. The exact wording of the instructions and test items follows:

> Let's suppose that you are a *public official* who has to decide how much money each program should get.
> Let's say that the people who run these programs have come to you saying that they each need $100,000 extra to pay for their programs. The problem is that you have only $100,000 *total* to give *all* these different programs. (At this point, the interviewer hands the respondent 20 $5,000 bills.)
> We'd like you to divide the money among all of the 7 programs according to how important you think the individual programs are. (The interviewer now lays out a card display with the names of the seven groups, and asks the respondent to divide the money among the groups.)

To achieve some fit between the service and welfare group in question, the services in any one category were not totally identical. Thus, for transportation the services for which respondents allocated funds were: "special bus services for physically disabled persons over 65"; "half price bus fares to poor people over 65"; "special bus services for physically disabled persons under 65"; half price bus fares to poor people under 65"; special bus services for physically disabled children"; "half price bus fares for poor children"; and "special transportation services for victims of natural disasters right after disasters." As can be seen, the strategy was to keep the wording as similar as possible across all the services within a particular category, but permitting deviations required by the intrinsic differences between being, say, poor versus physically disabled.

The questions within the education category may give a better understanding of the wording, since the education questions were asked first and the interviewer read more background information. The relevant services were: "Information and referral center for people over 65 who are physically disabled. These were set up to inform them about programs which they are eligible for and to help them apply for benefits." "Information and referral centers for people over 65 who are poor. These were set up to inform them about services which they are eligible for, and also to show them how to apply for benefits." "Rehabilitation and job training programs for physically disabled people under 65. These have been set up to help disabled people get and keep jobs." "Job training programs. These have been set up for poor people under 65 to educate and train them so that they can get jobs." "Head Start programs for poor children. These have been set up to give them special attention before they start school so that they will not have so much trouble later." "Special education programs for physically disabled children. These have been set up to help them cope with their handicaps so that they can remain in regular schools with other children their own age." "Information and education services for victims of natural disasters, such as floods, hurricanes or tornadoes. These have been set up to help natural disaster victims learn how to repair the damage done and how to apply for programs they might be eligible for."

Similar instructions to those just reported were also given for the nutrition and income support services. For each service, the support measure was the amount of money the respondent assigned to each welfare group.

The general increase in services scale. Another measure of support was based on responses to the following question:

There are a number of services financed by the federal government to provide for some of the needs of each of these seven groups—for example, programs that provide money, food, or medical care. Some people feel there should be even *more* services for particular groups; other people feel there should be fewer programs. And other people, of course, have opinions somewhere in between.

We'd like to know how you feel about services financed by the federal government for the groups we've mentioned. First, let's consider people *over 65* who are poor. (Interviewer hands respondent a card with a 7 cell "services scale" on it.) If you feel that public programs and services for the elderly poor should be greatly increased, pick box 7. If you feel public programs should stay at the same level, pick box number 4. What box best describes your opinion? (Interviewer continues to ask about the remaining six welfare groups.)

Summary index. An index was also formed by standardizing each person's response for each of the four services in the money distribution measure and for the general services measure and then summing the five standardized scores.

The nutrition scale. Another measure of support was designed that did not require distributing simulated money. Instead, questions were asked verbally about willingness to pay higher taxes and write letters on behalf of a particular group. This measure involved questions about expanding, cutting back, or keeping at the same level a nutrition program for each of the seven welfare groups.

For each group the question about support was followed by three items designed to explore the respondents' level of commitment to their position. First, they were asked how strongly they felt about their response to cut back, expand, or keep the same level of the program. Responses were coded from one to seven. Second, they were asked how willing they would be to sign a petition to someone in government stating their point of view. Again, the responses were scored from one to seven. Finally, they were asked how much more they would be willing to pay in taxes if the only way the program could be enlarged was by raising taxes. Here the response alternatives were "no more, $1 more for every $100 you already pay, $3 more for every $100 you already pay, $5 more for every $100 you already pay." To convert this final question into a seven part scale as were the others, the four alternatives above were coded as 4 through 7, and the very strong, fairly strong, and not too strong feelings in favor of cutbacks from question one were treated as the responses 1 through 3.

Since each of the three main questions that rate strength of commitment to the program has answers that form a 1 to 7 scale, a composite scale was constructed. This was achieved by simply adding the answers to all the three questions.

Measures of Potential Explanatory Variables

The potential explanatory variables we measured were: (1) the respondents' level of belief in a just world; (2) their perception of the likelihood of a social welfare group's plight happening to them; (3) whether they knew a member of a particular welfare group; (4) whether they had received government aid; (5) how they perceived the welfare group's need; (6) the group's deservingness; (7) pleasantness; (8) gratefulness; and (9) whether they perceived the group as responsible for its plight. We now discuss each of these measures in turn.

Belief in a just world. The level of belief in a just world was measured by a revised version of the Just World Scale developed by Rubin (1975). Rubin's measure is a 20-item paper-

and-pencil self-administered scale. The index used in the present study was a modification of Rubin's in two respects. Rather than the respondents reading and scoring each item themselves, interviewers read the items to them. This change was made to standardize the experience for respondents as much as possible since some respondents were too poorly educated and had too poor eyesight to read and score the items.

Second, because the original 20 items took too long to read to respondents in a one-hour interview that included many other questions, the scale was shortened to 10 items. The item selection was made on the basis of a study with 168 undergraduate students attending the Chicago Circle Campus of the University of Illinois. They completed the 20-item Belief in a Just World Scale as a part of a larger questionnaire concerned with social comparison, relative deprivation, and feelings of unfairness. These students were from a variety of ethnic and racial backgrounds and were from 17 to 42 years old. (Most were from 18 to 22 years old.) These responses were analyzed and the questions with the highest interitem correlations were selected for use in the survey reported here.

Likelihood of the respondent entering one of the social welfare groups. This was measured by the following question:

Though none of us knows definitely what will happen to us in the near future, most of us have a fairly good idea of how *likely* we are to face certain kinds of problems in life—such as becoming disabled or being a victim of a natural disaster. In this section, we'd like to find out how likely you think it is that you might have to deal with some of the problems that we've asked about before.

First, let's take the problem of being a victim of a natural disaster, such as a flood or tornado. How likely is it that something like this might happen to you? Would you say practically no chance, possible but not very likely, there's a 50-50 chance, it's very likely, or you are already in this situation. (Interviewer hands respondent card with 1-5 likelihood scale on it.)

Belonging to one of the welfare groups. This was measured in two ways. The first was the fifth category of the above question. The respondent could say that he or she was "already in the situation" of a particular welfare group. In addition, background demographic characteristics were collected on each person—age, income, health status. These data permitted us to test whether, for example, the elderly poor were more in favor of programs for the elderly, the nonelderly for the nonelderly, and the poor for the poor.

Knowing members of a welfare group. This was measured by asking the respondent at the end of the interview whether or not he or she has a "relative or close friend who might fit into one of the groups we have been discussing." Responses were recorded as "yes" or "no" for knowing a member of each welfare group.

Prior receipt of government aid. This was measured by the answer to the question: "Did you ever—because of sickness, unemployment, or any other reason—receive anything like AFDC, unemployment insurance, or other aid from government agencies?" Responses were coded as "yes" or "no." If the answer was "yes," interviewers listed the type of aid received.

The perceived need of each welfare group. The level of need of a group was measured by where respondents placed a welfare group on a hypothetical "ladder of life." This ladder was developed by Cantril (1965) to measure socioeconomic aspirations. A rating of ten is considered "the best possible life," and a rating of zero the "worst possible life." Respondents were asked to rate where each of the seven social welfare groups stand on the ladder *at present* and where they stood *five years ago.*

Perceived deservingness, gratefulness, and pleasantness of each welfare group. These concepts were measured by the respondents' answers to a self-administered semantic differential consisting of three bipolar rating scales applied to each of the seven groups: (1) deserving-undeserving; (2) grateful-ungrateful; (3) pleasant-unpleasant.

Perceived locus of responsibility. This was also measured by means of responses to a semantic differential item where the poles were "hardship own fault" and "hardship not own fault." Responses were obtained for each of the welfare groups.

EXPERIMENTAL DESIGN

Overall Design

In principle, the experiment was simple enough. It seemed reasonable to assume that an individual's support for government aid programs for disadvantaged people might depend upon the particular *characteristics of the individual respondent*—more specifically his or her age, race, sex, and income—and also upon the *characteristics of the person in need*—more specifically his or her age (over or under sixty-five), the nature of his or her condition (poor versus disabled), the severity of this condition (absent, present at marginal levels, present at high acute levels, and present at high chronic levels), and the reason for his or her being in this condition (self-caused versus other-caused).[2] The full experimental design dealing with characteristics of the persons in need is outlined in Table 2.2.

The Manipulations

To operationalize these characteristics of welfare group members, brief vignettes were written describing a "disadvantaged" person. The attributes of this person had been carefully tailored to meet the explanatory requirements of the experiment. To illustrate, below is a vignette in which the character is chronically poor, chronically disabled, and young. His poverty and disability were caused by forces beyond his control.

James Richards is 32 years old. He has always been very poor without enough income to buy adequate food and clothing. Although he tried hard, he could never get into a job training program to acquire skills for a steady job. So, all he's been able to find are odd jobs around town.

A few weeks ago, he was the victim of a hit-and-run driver. The accident left him permanently paralyzed from the waist down. For the rest of his life, it will be extremely difficult for him to take care of himself and his apartment.

In the next vignette, the individual is also chronically poor and chronically disabled, but these conditions were self-caused.

Charles Robinson is 31 years old. Again this week he won't be able to pay his rent. He is very poor and has been poor nearly all his life because he can never find a job he wants to stay with for more than a few months.

A few weeks ago, he caused an accident by driving carelessly in a rainstorm and wrecked his car. He was seriously injured and both his legs will be permanently paralyzed. Since he lives alone, he will have a very difficult time getting around on his own and trying to care for himself and his apartment.

Note that the conditions of chronic poverty and chronic disability have been described in similar ways for both James Richards and Charles Robinson. What varies is the responsibility for the conditions. In the first case, Richards was poor but he had "tried hard" and "could never get into a job training program." In the second case, Robinson was poor because he could not find a job with which he wanted to stay. There were also differences in who was responsible for their disability: Richards was a victim of a hit-and-run driver, while Robinson caused an accident while driving carelessly.

In the vignettes, care was taken to vary only the characteristics under study. Above, only "responsibility for plight" was varied, while the plight itself stayed the same. In other vignettes, only the age of the individual varied; that is, individuals similar to Richards and Robinson were described but with one difference: They were in their late sixties or early seventies. In still other vignettes, the individuals were poor but had no disability or they were disabled but not poor. Table 2.2 demonstrates how the levels of the four vignette factors of poverty (none, marginal, acute, chronic); disability (none, marginal, acute, chronic); age (young adult, elderly adult); and responsibility for plight (self-caused, other-caused) were factorially combined to give a total of 64 separate vignettes (4 levels of poverty times 4 levels of disability times 2 age levels times 2 responsibility conditions).

The complete set of vignettes is in Cook (1977). There are so many they cannot be presented here. However, we can present the guidelines for operationalizing poverty, physical disability, and locus of causality for plight.

High Chronic Disability (Permanent)—Disability prevents individual from walking upstairs, moving about, doing ordinary chores around the house. The areas of activity that are extremely limited or missing are:

a. Mobility: walking, negotiating stairs, transfer in and out of bed or chairs, and travel.

b. Self-care: feeding, dressing, and toilet care.

c. Domestic duties: shopping, preparation and cooking of food, household cleaning, washing of clothes.

Table 2.2: Four-Factor Experimental Design

Age of Vignette Subjects	Locus of Causality	Extent of Disability	Extent of Poverty			
			None	*Marginal*	*High Acute*	*High Chronic*
< 65	Self	None Marginal High acute High chronic				
	Other	None Marginal High acute High chronic				
65 +	Self	None Marginal High acute High chronic				
	Other	None Marginal High acute High chronic				

d. Occupation: the ability to hold unmodified employment in open industry consistent with the individual's age, sex, and skill.

High Acute Disability (Temporary)—Disability prevents individual from the above activities for a limited time period—say, about six months or less than a year. However, the condition will not continue.

Marginal Disability—Some activities listed above are restricted, but individual can manage. He is, therefore, only marginally incapacitated.

No Disability—Individual is depicted as healthy and able-bodied.

High Chronic Poverty (Permanent)—The available money is not enough to pay for the minimum needs of housing, food, and clothing. There are no savings.

High Acute Poverty (Temporary)—The condition of poverty is the same as the above chronic condition but it will last for only a limited time period—about six months.

Marginal Poverty—There is only enough money for the basic minimum needs of housing, food, and clothing but never any left over for extras.

No Poverty—There is both enough money for the basic minimum needs listed above and for extras such as vacations and entertainment.

The operationalization of locus of causality had to vary with the age of the vignette character, and Table 2.3 may give an intuitive understanding of how age and locus of causality were manipulated. It can be seen from Table 2.3 that poverty is a combination of work history and/or current employment (income) and expenses which must be met (outflow). Thus, the cause of poverty was slightly different for retired people over 65 than it was for people under 65. On the other hand, the cause of disability was the same regardless of age.

Table 2.3: Guidelines for Operationalizing Locus of Causality

Poverty Level	Self-Caused	Other-Caused
	Young Person (30s)	
Marginal	The person is under-employed and rejects chance for improvement	The person is under-employed and tries to improve but can't get a chance to improve
High Acute	Severe added expenses due to self Recent loss of job due to self. Other job won't start for six months	Severe added expenses due to others Recent loss of job due to business failure not related to self
High Chronic	Chronic unemployment Won't take jobs offered	Chronic unemployment Can't get job, though he tries
	Old Person (late 60s, early 70s)	
Marginal	Low Social Security because of his low income during working years in which he rejected chances for advancement	Low Social Security because of under-employment during working years in which he had no opportunity to improve
High Acute	Heavy added expense due to self, plus low Social Security because of rejection of chance for improvement during working years	Heavy added expense due to self, plus low Social Security because of bad job market in his area during his working years
	No Social Security (only SSI) because person would not take job during working years	No Social Security (only SSI) because person wasn't able to get jobs
Disability Level	*Any Age Person*	
Marginal	Was driving. Wasn't looking where he was going. Or similar situation of careless-ness	Struck by a hit-and-run driver or driver who ran a stop sign or drunken driver, etc.
High Acute	Same type cause as above	Same type cause as above
High Chronic	Same type cause as above	Same type cause as above

The Deliberate Confounding Plan

If each of the 384 respondents was presented with an identical set of different vignettes and his or her "level of support" for government aid programs for the vignette character was then measured, we could accomplish two goals. First, we could compare support among respondents who differed by age, race, sex, and income. This would enable us to learn, for example, whether there are differences between blacks and whites in "welfare support." We could also learn whether any such differences would disappear, persist, or even increase depending upon the income, age, or sex of black and white respondents. Second, we could compare to what extent welfare support depends on such characteristics of welfare group members as level of poverty, level of disability, age, or level of responsibility for being in a welfare group. Table 2.2 has shown how various levels of these four factors combine to result in a total of 64 separate vignettes.

A factorial design with independent observations in each cell presents the unattractive prospect of exposing each respondent to all 64 vignettes. This could not be done because of the physical constraints of a one-hour interview format, and also because we felt no respondent would (or could) tolerate answering the same battery of support questions after each of 64 vignettes. Faced with the need to reduce the number of experimental treatments presented to each respondent, we turned to an "incomplete-within-blocks" design. Basically, this allows a relaxation of the requirement to present all possible combinations of all treatment levels to all respondents at the cost of deliberately measuring some higher-order interactions with less precision than others. After complex mathematical formulations, and some a priori decisions about which interaction effects were less important to measure with maximum precision, we were able to construct a set of rules for assigning a reduced set of treatment combinations to our respondents.

Instead of presenting all sixty-four experimental vignettes to each individual respondent, we developed a logically balanced procedure for presenting each respondent with only eight vignettes.[3] The balancing procedure guaranteed that each respondent would experience four vignettes describing "young" subjects as well as four vignettes depicting "old" subjects; four in which subjects caused their own needy situation and four in which they were blameless; and two vignettes depicting subjects at each of the four levels of both poverty and disability. But in a given block of eight respondents, each would experience *different combinations* of the treatment levels. In this way, all sixty-four possible combinations were distributed systematically across the eight respondents in each of the twenty-four blocks of individual respondent variables (i.e., the blocks formed by combining two levels of race, age, and sex with three levels of income as depicted in Table 2.1.

Since there were not eight but sixteen respondents in each of these blocks, we were able to carry out the experiment in *two replications,* with a second set of twenty-four blocks of eight respondents and a different but equally systematic balancing of treatment levels within each block. An important point to note is that any effect that was deliberately confounded in one replication was not confounded in the other. Thus, every effect had at least one unbiased test. To help the reader understand the complex experiment, Appendix 2 contains a detailed exposition of the deliberate confounding plan.

Measures of Support

In the experiment, the respondents were asked a series of five questions after each vignette about their support for the vignette character. The responses were coded as yes, no, or don't know.

(1) Do you have any sympathy for (vignette character's name) and the situation he is in?

(2) Do you think it's important to have services financed by the federal government to help people in situations like (vignette character's name) is in? (If no, go to next vignette.) (If yes, ask questions 3-5.)

(3) There are a number of things which people can do to support service programs to help people in conditions like (vignette character's name). One might be to sign a petition or write a letter to someone who is responsible for such programs.

Would you sign a petition or write a letter to someone in government supporting such programs?

(4) Another way might be to attend a local public meeting to demonstrate support for programs to help people in conditions like (vignette character's name) is in. Would you attend such a meeting?

(5) Suppose that services for people like (vignette character's name) couldn't be supplied unless taxes were raised. Would you be willing to pay slightly higher taxes to support programs to help people like him?

At the outset, we hypothesized that responses to these five questions would vary unidimensionally representing the underlying construct of "support." In addition, we hoped to be able to capture some sense of the level or intensity of that support by using a series of items, each of which was presumed to reflect a stronger commitment to support. For instance, saying one would write a letter to someone in government about a program is more difficult than saying one has sympathy for a person. And saying one would be willing to pay higher taxes is more difficult than writing a letter. The analysis below reveals, we believe, that we are justified in using as our primary dependent measure of level of support, a standardized, weighted sum of the positive responses to our five separate support questions.

First, in order to confirm that our five support items did indeed tap a unitary dimension, a series of principal components factor analyses was performed on the responses to the five items. This was done in two forms: (1) separately for each set of five scores following each of the eight experimental vignettes, and (2) using average item scores taken across the eight vignettes. In each case, a single, unambiguous "support" factor emerged. The relevant eigenvalues and the proportions of total variance which the five items explained are reported in Cook (1977).

Second, by constructing a series of increasingly higher barriers to expressions of support, we hoped to be able to differentiate between respondents on a "support intensity" continuum. The data suggest that we were partly successful in accomplishing our aim. Table 2.4 displays the percentages of the sample giving positive or supportive responses to each of the five support questions, both separately for each of the eight vignettes and also averaged over all eight vignettes. These data clearly show that the first three items present increasingly greater obstacles to support (fewer respondents respond supportively to the government support item than to the sympathy question and fewer still for the writing/petitioning item than for the government support question). However, the meeting and tax questions, though they present higher obstacles than the first three questions, cannot be distinguished from one another in terms of the apparent difficulty of making a supportive response. Thus, although these results show that we have not captured a five-item gradated hierarchy of support intensity, we can nevertheless create a single summary measure called *level of support,* based on a weighted sum of the five items, with the "meeting" and tax items having roughly equal weights. The only question remaining is what the specific values of each item's weight should be.

We chose to assign weights to the five items based upon estimates of conditional probabilities that respondents would express support on the *more difficult* questions, given a prior supportive response to an easier question.[4] First, to average out responses across all eight vignettes, a respondent was classified as *supportive* on a particular item if he responded

Table 2.4:   Percentage of Repondents Giving Supportive Responses to
Each of Five Support Questions

Vignette	Feel Sympathy	Government Finance	Write or Petition	Attend Meeting	Pay Higher Taxes
1	85	79	66	51	52
2	76	70	59	43	42
3	75	67	56	45	41
4	80	69	58	44	42
5	72	62	52	41	40
6	74	62	53	39	40
7	66	59	50	35	37
8	76	65	56	38	39
Average	76	67	56	42	42

positively to that item for at least five of the eight vignette
treatments. Next, using simple cross-tabulations, a series of
conditional probabilities was estimated for the second
through fifth items, given supportive responses to each previous item. These estimates are contained in Table 2.5. Reading across the first row, respondents classified as supportive
on the "sympathy" question have a probability of .76 of
being favorable to government-financed programs for the
vignette subject, a probability of .63 of showing willingess to
sign a petition or write a letter to someone in government, a
probability of .46 of expressing willingness to attend a public
meeting, and .47 of being willing to pay higher taxes. Likewise, those who respond positively to the government finance
question have a .80 probability of expressing support on the
write/petition item, a probability of .58 of indicating willingness to attend a public meeting, and so on. Because the
meeting and tax items appeared to be about equal in difficulty, conditional probabilities were estimated for each of
these measures with respect to the other.

Actual weights were computed from these probabilities as
follows. First, a respondent was given an arbitrary score of 10
if he expressed sympathy for the subject of an experimental

Table 2.5: Estimates of Conditional Probabilities for More Difficult
           Acts of Support, Based on Support for Easier Acts[a]

Item	Government Finance	Write or Petition	Attend Meeting	Pay Higher Taxes	Attend Meeting
Feel sympathy	.76	.63	.46	.47	–
Government finance		.80	.58	.60	–
Write or petition			.70	.69	–
Attend meeting				.74	–
Pay higher taxes					.71

a. Table entries are sample proportions giving supportive responses to items designated in both row and column headings.

vignette. A respondent who supported government programs
for the vignette subject received a score computed as a
product of the *base score* (10) multiplied by a *difficulty
factor* (in this case, the reciprocal of the conditional probability which constrains it, namely $1/.76 = 1.32$) for a total of
13.2. Computing weights for the remaining three items is
made slightly more complex by the fact that there are multiple conditional probabilities associated with their occurrence. For example, for the "write/petition" item *two* separate weights can be estimated from the conditional probabilities associated with both prior questions, the "sympathy" and "government finance" items. Weights for the
"meeting" and "pay tax" items must be computed from
eight separate estimates of the conditional probabilities of
their occurrence. For each of the last three items, final
weights were arrived at by averaging over multiple estimates.
Finally, weighted item scores were standardized to cover a
range from 0 (no supportive responses toward the vignette
subject) to 100 (five supportive responses). This procedure

Table 2.6: Weights and Scores for Five Individual Support Items Used in Computing Composite "Level of Support" Scores

Item	Base	x	Weight	=	Weighted Score	Rescaled Score
Feel sympathy	10		1.00		10.0	10.7
Government finance	10		1.32		13.2	14.2
Write/petition	10		1.62		16.2	17.4
Attend meeting	10		2.72		27.2	29.2
Pay higher taxes	10		2.66		26.6	28.5
					Total	100.0

led to the item weights and scores reported in Table 2.6. The important point to note about the index is that scores are weighted so as to make the behavioroid measures of willingness to pay more taxes and to attend a meeting count considerably more than the other measures.

Statistical Testing in the Experiment

With 384 respondents whose age, race, sex, and income could be used as stratification variables, with multiple observations from each respondent on eight vignette characters, and with a highly reliable index of support, it should not be surprising to learn that the statistical power of the experiment is considerable, far greater than for any of the tests using data from the traditional part of the survey. Indeed, we shall later learn that effects in the experiment could be statistically significant even if they accounted for only 1/10 of 1 percent of the variance in the support index!

Rather than using conventional hypotheses-testing strategies for the statistical evaluation of the results from the experiment, we decided to use magnitude estimation as our means of deciding which effects were practically significant. Hence, for each effect we calculated Hays ω^2 (omega squared), a measure of the variance accounted for; and we specified $\omega^2 < .01$ as the cutting point; that is, an effect had to account for 1 percent of the variance in support to be considered worth discussing. Note that this is 1 percent of the variance that can be accounted for, and that not all of the variance can be accounted for since random error limits the accountable variance to less than 100 percent.

NOTES

1. An alternative decision could have been made to deal with the income differentiation between blacks and whites. We could have stratified black and white census tracts according to the same income cut-offs. Even though there were no predominantly black census tracts with median incomes above $19,558, interviewers could have screened households until they found blacks with the upper bound of that median figure. This approach was not chosen because of fiscal constraints: it is simply too expensive for interviewers who are paid by the hour to continue going from house to house until they track down people who form such a relatively small segment of the population. In addition, it can be argued that "low, middle, and high income" are different in the black community as opposed to the white community because of the "real world" differences between the two, however unfortunate and intolerable these may be.

2. The race of the vignette character was not specified. Race was not one of the traits of welfare groups being experimentally manipulated.

3. Special thanks to Dr. Albert Erlebacher, Associate Professor, Psychology Department, Northwestern University, for his help in developing this procedure and to Calvin C. Jones, Political Science Department, University of Chicago, for his help in implementing it.

4. We are indebted to Calvin Jones for suggesting this use of conditional probabilities.

Chapter 3

THE PUBLIC'S SUPPORT FOR WELFARE GROUPS

This chapter addresses the question: what are the differences in level of support for government-financed social services for poor children, disabled children, poor adults under 65, disabled adults under 65, poor elderly persons, disabled elderly persons, and disaster victims? Assumptions are often made about those groups for whom the general public is willing to provide tax-financed services. However, as we saw in Chapter 1, these assumptions are often contradictory. Some hold that children are the most favored group, while others cite the elderly and still others cite disaster victims.

Assumptions are also made that most members of the general public have a prioritized *ranking* of welfare groups they are willing to support and that these ranks are invariant, applying to all social services. Hidden behind this assumption is the idea that the public is not very discerning about which groups should be supported most, and instead bases its opinion upon general, probably stereotypical notions about the groups.

The design of this study allows the above assumptions to be tested in two separate contexts. One is in a traditional survey, and the other is as part of an experiment embedded in the questionnaire. In the traditional survey part of the study, respondents distributed simulated money among the seven groups for four social services—nutrition, income guarantees, transportation, and education. They also rated how much support they would give for more services in general; and they responded to questions about cutbacks and willingness to pay more taxes for nutrition services for each of the groups. If a person has a set priority system of preferentially supporting the groups, then we would expect that his ranking system would be the same regardless of the service in question. On the other hand, if a person is discerning and links the nature of the service to certain characteristics and needs of the group, then we would expect his willingness to support a group to vary according to the service in question.

In the experimental part of the study, the interviewer presented the respondents with vignettes describing elderly poor persons, elderly disabled persons, disabled adults under 65, or poor adults under 65. Then questions were asked about how much the respondent would want to support the person described, including support by paying higher taxes.

SUPPORT FINDINGS FROM THE SURVEY

Support for Specific Programs

For transportation, the specific services in question were: special buses for disabled persons who were over 65, under 65, or children; half price fares for the poor over 65, under 65, or children; and special transportation for disaster victims immediately after the disaster.

The mean amounts of money distributed by the respondents are displayed in Table 3.1. The subscript system used will be employed throughout the rest of this chapter's tables. Subscripts indicate which groups are supported more than each other group at the .05 significance level. Thus, disabled children are ranked as group 1 and there is a subscript 1 after each group beginning with the third-ranked "disabled adults under 65." This means that more support is given to disabled children than to all the groups ranked three or below. If there is no subscript, this means that the groups in question are not differently supported to a statistically significant degree. In reporting results derived from combining individual groups, e.g. in contrasting the elderly (both disabled and poor) with adults under 65 (disabled and poor), we shall report significance levels in the text.

Table 3.1 shows a clear preference for helping the disabled over the poor. Indeed, the average difference in support between these two groups is about $3,500. Although the disability-poverty distinction seems to be the most important criterion of support for transportation programs, it is also possible to explore respondents' age group preferences. Overall, the elderly are assigned the most funds (average support, about $15,000); next come children (average support just over $14,000; p difference from the elderly < .05); and last come adults under 65 (average support about $12,500; p difference from children < .001). Disaster victims are among the least likely to be supported, receiving $11,150. Poor adults under 65 receive the lowest support of all ($9,950).

For *nutrition* programs, the specific services mentioned for each group were: meals-on-wheels for the disabled over 65 and under 65; food stamps for the poor over 65 and under 65; school lunch programs for poor and disabled children; and food assistance programs for disaster victims.

The mean amount of money distributed to each group is indicated in Table 3.2. Respondents seem to focus first on age as a decisive criterion of support rather than the poverty-disability distinction. Highest priority goes to the elderly (average support about $16,300), who are preferred over children (average about $12,200; p difference < .001) and adults under 65 (average about $12,600; p difference from elderly < .001). As far as the disability-poverty distinction is

Table 3.1:   Mean Levels of Money Distributed for
             Transportation Services

Rank	Group	Mean[a]
(1)	Disabled children	$16,050
(2)	Disabled elderly	15,900
(3)	Disabled adults under 65[1, 2]	15,000
(4)	Poor elderly [1, 2, 3]	13,800
(5)	Poor children[1, 2, 3, 4]	12,250
(6)	Disaster victims[1, 2, 3, 4, 5]	11,150
(7)	Poor adults under 65[1, 2, 3, 4, 5, 6]	9,950
	Mean	$13,450
	Standard deviation	2,650

a. Taking every possible comparison between groups, correlated
t-tests were performed to determine if the difference between the
means was significant at the .05 level. The subscripts indicate the
groups with whom comparisons were statistically significant.

concerned, the poor and disabled elderly do not significantly
differ; poor children are preferred to disabled children to a
small but statistically significant degree (respective means =
$13,350 versus $12,300) while disabled persons under 65 are
greatly preferred over poor persons under 65 (respective
means = $14,250 versus $11,100). Poor adults under 65
receive the least support of all.

For a guaranteed minimum income, the interviewer read:
"If an individual is not able to work full time, is not able to
work at all, or does not receive sufficient income from
private means, then (through a guaranteed minimum income
program) he is guaranteed an income by the federal government. This would be the minimum amount necessary to buy
food and clothing and to pay for housing." The interviewer
then asked the respondents to allocate simulated money to
each group, mentioning only the group's name. An exception
was made for the two groups of children where the interviewer added that the money would have to go to the parents
or the person who cares for the child.

Table 3.2: Mean Levels of Money Distribution for
            Nutrition Services

Rank	Group	Mean
(1)	Disabled elderly	$16,750
(2)	Poor elderly	15,900
(3)	Disabled adults under 65$_{1,2}$	14,250
(4)	Poor children$_{1,2}$	13,350
(5)	Disabled children$_{1,2,3,4}$	12,300
(6)	Disaster victims$_{1,2,3,4}$	11,850
(7)	Poor adults under 65$_{1,2,3,4,5}$	11,100
	Mean	$13,650
	Standard deviation	2,300

The mean amounts of money distributed are shown in
Table 3.3. The most striking feature of the table is that the
elderly (average support = $15,075) are preferred for support
over other age groups (p difference from children and adults
under 65 < .001), with the disabled elderly ($16,100) pre-
ferred over the poor elderly ($14,050).

It is difficult to decide whether respondents focus more on
age than condition. Although the most preferred groups are
both elderly, all three groups of the physically disabled are in
the highest ranks. The groups that respondents are clearly
least likely to support for guaranteed income programs are
poor adults under 65 ($10,450) and disaster victims
($9,100); these groups have consistently received the least
support across all the programs discussed so far.

However, poor adults under 65 are assigned the very highest priority for funds for *education programs*. The programs
proposed were: information and referral centers for disaster
victims, for the elderly poor, and the elderly disabled to help
them learn of, and apply for, benefits to which they were
entitled; job-training programs were specified for adults
under 65 (with a rehabilitation component for the disabled)
to help them gain and maintain employment; Head Start

Table 3.3:   Mean Levels of Money Distribution for Income
             Services

Rank	Group	Mean
(1)	Disabled elderly	$16,100
(2)	Poor Elderly $_1$	14,050
(3)	Disabled adults under 65$_1$	14,000
(4)	Disabled children$_1$	13,600
(5)	Poor children$_{1, 2, 3, 4}$	12,000
(6)	Poor adults under 65$_{1, 2, 3, 4, 5}$	10,450
(7)	Disaster victims$_{1, 2, 3, 4, 5, 6}$	9,100
	Mean	$12,750
	Standard deviation	3,280

programs were proposed for poor children to help them do
better in school, while special education classes were proposed for disabled children to help them stay in regular
schools.

The sums assigned to each group are given in Table 3.4.
Age is clearly the major factor in determining support and for
the first time adults under 65 (average support about
$16,000) received significantly more support than the elderly
(average support about $12,800; p difference < .001) and
children (average support = $14,200; p difference from adults
under 65 < .001). The reason may be that the description of
education programs for poor and disabled adults under 65
states that they will be educated and trained for jobs, and
jobs were not referred to in describing the purpose of education programs for children or the elderly.[1] The next groups to
receive support for education programs are children—first
disabled children and then poor children. For the first time in
this study, children as an age group receive significantly more
support than the elderly (p < .001). Receiving the least support are disaster victims.

Table 3.4:   Mean Levels of Money Distribution for
             Education Services

Rank	Group	Mean
(1)	Poor adults under 65	$16,200
(2)	Disabled adults under 65	15,750
(3)	Disabled children	15,250
(4)	Poor children$_{1, 2, 3}$	13,200
(5)	Disabled elderly $_{1, 2, 3}$	13,100
(6)	Poor elderly $_{1, 2, 3, 4}$	12,500
(7)	Disaster victims$_{1, 2, 3, 4, 5, 6}$	9,750
	Mean	$13,700
	Standard deviation	2,400

Generalized Support for Services

Respondents were also asked to indicate the extent to which they thought *general social services* financed by tax dollars should be increased or decreased for each of the seven welfare groups. On this scale a score of one indicates the belief that services should be decreased, while a score of seven means services should be increased and a midpoint score is interpreted as a belief that services should stay at the same level. Overall, more support goes to services for the disabled (mean = 5.98) than for the poor (mean = 5.47; p difference < .001). Among the three age groups, most support is assigned to services for the elderly (mean = 5.90); significantly less support is given to services for children (mean = 5.75, p difference < .01); and least support goes to services for adults under 65 (mean = 5.48). Indeed, the support for adults under 65 is significantly less than that for both the elderly (p < .001) and children (p < .001). Support for any age group appears to depend on whether that group is disabled or poor. At any age, more support exists for those who are disabled than for those who are poor. Disaster

Table 3.5: Mean Levels of Support for a General Increase
in Services

Rank	Group	Mean
(1)	Disabled children	6.05
(2)	Disabled elderly	6.02
(3)	Disabled adults under 65	5.87
(4)	Poor elderly $_{1, 2, 3}$	5.79
(5)	Disaster victims $_{1, 2, 3}$	5.62
(6)	Poor children $_{1, 2, 3}$	5.54
(7)	Poor adults under 65 $_{1, 2, 3, 4, 5, 6}$	5.09
	Mean	5.73
	Standard deviation	1.04

victims rank higher on this particular global measure of
support than on any other scale, even though only support
for poor adults under 65 is reliably less than support for
disaster victims.

A *support index* was constructed across all services for
each group to determine in an overall way how the respondents differentiated among the groups. Table 3.6 shows how
much support each welfare group receives when the responses
to all the support questions we have presented thus far are
standardized and summed to form a general index of support.

Overall, the disabled receive more support than the poor,
occupying the first three ranks. Disaster victims are supported least, and the degree of support is reliably less than
for all other groups. Among the disabled, the elderly receive
most support, followed by adults under 65. Children receive
significantly less support than the elderly and adults under
65. Among the poor, the elderly again receive most support;
children receive significantly less support than the elderly;
and adults under 65 receive significantly less support than
both the elderly and children.

Table 3.6: Overall Level of Support for Seven Social
Welfare Groups (General Support Index,
Standardized)

Rank	Group	Mean
(1)	Disabled elderly	2.87
(2)	Disabled adults under 65	2.35
(3)	Disabled children[1]	1.70
(4)	Poor elderly [1, 2]	.89
(5)	Poor children[1, 2, 3, 4]	-1.06
(6)	Poor adults under 65[1, 2, 3, 4, 5]	-2.25
(7)	Disaster victims[1, 2, 3, 4, 5, 6]	-3.85
	Mean	0
	Standard deviation	1

Support on the Action-Oriented Nutrition Measure

The specific nutritional services that were used to measure support by having respondents distribute simulated money were also used to measure support by asking respondents if they wanted increases or decreases in such programs, how strongly they felt about this, how willing they would be to write their congressman about their opinion, and—if appropriate—by how much they would be prepared to have their taxes raised for the service in question. The responses were coded so as to generate a directional support index, and results for that index are given in Table 3.7. We shall call it the action scale since the last two items deal with anticipated future action.

The results show that the elderly and disabled are preferred over the younger persons and the poor. The only exception is if the disabled person is a child, in which case the least strong feelings and the least willingness to anticipate actions are reported. Another striking feature of Table 3.7 is

Table 3.7: Support for Nutrition Services on the Action
            Scale

Rank	Group	Mean
(1)	Disabled elderly	15.96
(2)	Poor elderly	15.58
(3)	Disabled adults under 65	15.48
(4)	Disaster victims$_{1, 2, 3}$	14.02
(5)	Poor children$_{1, 2, 3, 4}$	13.63
(6)	Poor adults under 65$_{1, 2, 3, 4, 5}$	12.71
(7)	Disabled children$_{1, 2, 3, 4, 5, 6}$	12.24
	Mean	14.23
	Standard deviation	1.00

the relatively high level of support volunteered for disaster
victims.

It is instructive to break down these results in order to
examine the component parts of the action support index.
The percentage of respondents wanting a decrease in current
levels of support is 4 percent or under for the elderly disabled, elderly poor, disabled under 65, and disaster victims.
The corresponding percentages for poor children, poor adults
under 65, and disabled children are 12, 24, and 21 percent.
The percentages wanting an expansion of services are disabled elderly, 70 percent; elderly poor, 65 percent; disabled
under 65, 63 percent; disaster victims, 36 percent; poor
children 43 percent; poor under 65, 40 percent; and disabled
children, 26 percent. The percentages willing to pay more
taxes are 63 percent for the elderly disabled, 38 percent for
the elderly poor, 58 percent for the disabled under 65, 23
percent for disaster victims, 27 percent for poor children, 22
percent for the poor under 65, and 17 percent for disabled
children.

We can now see, in particular, that disabled adults are
preferred for additional tax monies, but that disabled children are presumed to be the responsibility of agencies other

than the federal government (perhaps the family?). Also, while there is considerable abstract support for nutrition services for the elderly poor—who rank number two on both indexes of support for nutrition services—this support is reduced once respondents are asked to translate the support into tax dollars. Something similar happens with disaster victims. While support is surprisingly high for nutritional services for them on the action-oriented support index, this support is not translated into even one-quarter of the respondents reporting a willingness to increase their taxes. In short, the willingness to give nutritional support to the poor elderly and disaster victims seems to be "soft."

It is also instructive to compare the results for nutritional services with the money distribution measure (see Table 3.2) and the action-oriented measure (see Table 3.7). The elderly disabled and poor, and disabled adults under 65 have the same top rankings on each measure. Poor adults under 65 rank last and coequal last on each measure (coequal means not significantly different from a measure that may have had a different apparent rank). Poor children rank four on one measure and five on another; and disabled children rank last on one measure and coequal penultimate on another. The only discrepancy of any magnitude is for disaster victims, who, for the money distribution measure, are coequally penultimate, but for the action-oriented measure are ranked noticeably higher. This difference is not totally explicable, but it is worth noting that the support for disaster victims comes to rank lower once the action measure is to expand services or pay more taxes instead of the global support index. However, the possibility exists that low support for disaster victims is specific to the money distribution measures, since higher support is obtained for them with the one to seven scale for the measure of a general increase in social services (see Table 3.5). But for no measure are disaster victims in the top three groups to be supported.

Summary of the Survey Results

Two general conclusions seem warranted from the results we have examined thus far. First, in general, some welfare groups tend to be supported more than others. Disabled tend to be preferred over poor, elderly over children, and children over adults under 65. Probably the most preferred group consists of the elderly disabled and the least preferred of poor adults under 65 or disaster victims. The public does have preferences.

Second, although there are these general preferences, there are also distinct tendencies to make support for a group contingent on the nature of the service. Thus, disability is more powerful in determining support for transportation services than for other types of service; poor adults of working age are not at all supported for most services but are preferred to all others for job-related educational services; the disabled elderly are heavily preferred for income services and, to a lesser degree, for nutritional services but are among the least preferred for educational services. Although the public does have preferences, these preferences are not expressed undiscerningly. Rather, support for groups is made contingent on the service being provided from the public purse.

SUPPORT FINDINGS FROM THE VIGNETTES

Overview

The most interesting feature of the findings reported above is that the public's support for a group is contingent on the social service for which support was asked. But what if the respondent is not given a social service to consider for the group but rather is presented with a description of persons who fit into such groups and is then asked whether he or she would support tax-financed aid for such a person without the nature of the aid being specified. This situation existed in the experimental part of the study where respondents were given vignettes describing persons at different ages, with different levels of poverty and disability, and with different degrees of responsibility for their plight.

After hearing each vignette, respondents rated the extent to which (1) they had sympathy for the person in the vignette; (2) thought it was important to have tax-financed social services for such a person; (3) would sign a petition or write a letter to someone in government supporting service programs for people in such conditions; (4) would attend a local public meeting to demonstrate support for service programs for such people; and (5) would be willing to pay slightly higher taxes to support programs to help such people. The computation of support and scores was described in Chapter 2. We want to reiterate here that scores are weighted so as to make the "behavioroid" measures of willingness to pay more taxes, to attend a public meeting, and to write one's congressman count more than the other measures. Scores could range from 100, total support, to 0, no support at all.

Even after the creation of a single support scale, numerous support scores could be computed for each respondent: e.g., an average support score derived from the individual scores for each of the eight vignette characters, or particular support scores specific to vignettes about individuals who are disabled, poor, young, old, etc. It must be remembered that support scores for a specific group—say, for example, elderly people—include scores for elderly people who are disabled and poor as well as those who are not. This reduces comparability with the traditional survey part of the study since all the elderly in that part were presumably seen as needy in that they were either poor or disabled. None of the elderly could have been construed to be financially secure and in good health.

There were no children and no disaster victims in the vignettes. But there were marginally, chronically, and acutely poor elderly people; marginally, chronically, and acutely disabled elderly people; marginally, chronically, and acutely poor adults under 65; and marginally, chronically, and acutely disabled adults under 65. In addition, there were elderly persons and adults under 65 who were neither disabled nor poor.

Results

We present first the data on support for the disabled and poor persons summed across age and locus of the responsibility for the "victim's" plight. An analysis of variance showed that disabled persons receive more support than poor persons in every type of condition (marginal, acute, and chronic) as Figure 3.1 graphically illustrates. This replicates the general pattern found in the survey.

More importantly, perhaps, is the statistical interaction of poverty and disability (ω^2 = .03). This also is portrayed in

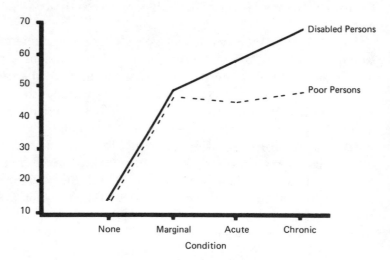

Figure 3.1: The interaction of poverty and disability

Figure 1, where it can be seen that the preference for helping the disabled over the poor is stronger the more serious the disability. This is a new effect that could not have been examined in the survey.

The analysis of the experimental data further shows that, in general, elderly persons receive significantly more support than younger persons ($\omega^2 = .01$). The mean support scores are 54.42 and 48.45 respectively. This difference also replicates the general pattern found in the nonexperimental section of the study.

Support may be separately compared for the young and elderly who are disabled or poor. Figures 3.2 and 3.3 show that elderly persons receive more help than younger persons in conditions of both poverty and disability. Whether the poverty and disability are chronic or acute seems to have some effect in mediating support. By superimposing Figures 3.2 and 3.3, we can see that if the person to be helped has a chronic condition, most support goes to the elderly disabled (62.42), followed by the young disabled (60.08), the elderly poor (56.44), and the young poor (51.09). This is exactly the preferential order found in the overall support index from the nonexperimental section of the survey. However, if the person to be helped has an acute condition, superimposing Figures 3.2 and 3.3 shows that most support still goes to the elderly disabled (58.32), but second most goes to the elderly poor (55.50), third most to the young disabled (51.93), and least to the young poor (50.67). The implication here is that in the traditional survey the respondents probably implicitly assumed that the disabled and poor persons to whom they were responding were chronically afflicted. Had they decided they were only temporarily afflicted, then the elderly poor might have received more support than they did. It is obvious, then, that chronic or acute affliction influences the support some groups are given.

For the most part, it appears (1) that within each age group, the disabled are preferred over the poor; and (2) that the elderly receive more support than adults under 65. These

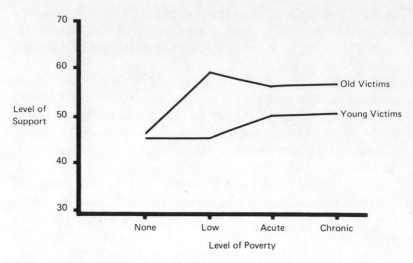

Figure 3.2: The interaction of poverty and age of victim

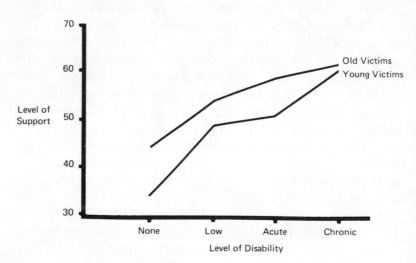

Figure 3.3: The interaction of disability and age of victim

findings emerge from two different types of research methodology—one a traditional survey format and the other an
experimental format using vignettes that varied the age and
condition of the person in need. It also appears that (3) the
preference for helping the disabled over the poor increases
with the level of seriousness of a disability; and (4) that the
elderly poor, in particular, receive more help relative to other
groups once it is decided they are acutely rather than chronically poor. These last two findings are unique to the experiment, since no comparable questions were asked in the survey.

CHAPTER SUMMARY

   Both the traditional survey and the experimental parts of
the study showed that, in general, the Chicago public prefers
to support some welfare groups more than others. The disabled are preferred over the poor, and it is likely that this
preference is greater the more serious the poverty and the
disability. Also, the elderly are preferred over children and
children over adults under 65. The public, in general, is most
willing to support the elderly disabled and least willing to
support poor adults under 65. In addition, the chronically
afflicted are likely to be supported more than the acutely
afflicted, particularly where disability is concerned. With our
Chicago population and the comparison groups we chose,
disaster victims have a distinctly low rating.
   These findings are less interesting than the finding that the
Chicago public is discerning in how it allocates aid. Although
it has preferences, these are not universal, applied willy-nilly
from one program to the next. Instead, support is made
contingent on the service being requested for a particular
group. Thus, the disabled consistently rank highest for trans-

portation services, and their preferred status for help is much less marked with income support programs. Poor adults under 65 are not popular for support for most types of services; but for education programs that involve job training they are the most preferred. Disabled children rank high for transportation and special education services, but rank among the very lowest for nutritional services that are presumably seen as the responsibility of some body other than the state. The elderly disabled rank highest of all for nutritional, income, and transportation services, but among the lowest for education services.

These findings suggest two further questions: (1) Is this discernment in the pattern of preferences shared by many of the subgroups within the Chicago sample studied, or is it merely a useless aggregate of many conflicting patterns of preference? (2) If the pattern of discernment is widespread, how can we elucidate the criteria that will help explain why some groups are relatively well supported for some services but not others and why different groups are well supported for quite different services? We will tackle the first of these questions in the next chapter, and the second question in Chapter 5.

NOTES

1. See the questionnaire in Appendix 1.
2. There was one unusual exception which can be seen when Figures 3.2 and 3.3 are compared. The marginally poor elderly received more support (mean = 58.74) than the disabled elderly (mean = 53.65) and the younger disabled (mean = 48.78).

Chapter 4

DIFFERENCES IN SUPPORT PATTERNS

WITHIN THE PUBLIC

INTRODUCTION

The Issue

The way in which different subgroups within the public differentiate among the seven welfare groups is the subject of this chapter. The aim here is to learn to what degree there is homogeneity or heterogeneity among population subgroups on the issue of support preference. Ideas from different academic disciplines lead one to expect that population subgroups will hold diverse views on a wide variety of issues due to the groups' different backgrounds, life styles, and ideologies. Two of these disciplines are marketing and political science.

In marketing research the concept of "segmentation" is of great importance. It refers to the fact that different kinds of persons (i.e., segments of the population) wish to consume different goods. Segmentation implies that advertisers would do well to discover which kinds of persons in the public are interested in their products, which media or interpersonal channels of communication members of the public use to learn about related types of products, and which types of persuasive appeal may be effective with the particular market segment interested in the product. Many reasons exist for the different purchasing patterns of different segments, some relating to acquired tastes, others to the particular needs associated with different stages in the life cycle, and still others to the financial resources available to a particular market segment for buying certain products.

A political science concept akin to market segmentation pervades much of the literature on political influence. Here, the stress is on "interest group politics." This refers to the inevitable conflicts of interest between some social groups and others and to the attempts by groups with common concerns to have policy-makers attend to their demands. The concept of interest group politics reflects the way Americans are often encouraged to think of themselves, i.e., as belonging to different membership groups within the population, whether these be occupational groups (e.g., farmers, physicians, teamsters), racial groups (black or Hispanic), political identifications (Democrat or Republican), or age groups (elderly, young adults, or children). The widespread presence of interest group politics serves, like the concept of segmentation in marketing, to remind us of differences in the American population, of the considerable heterogeneity of values, interests, tastes, needs, and resources within this nation.

This heterogeneity is also salient in public opinion research. When survey results are presented, either from public opinion polls or from more theory-oriented research, the data are invariably broken down by different types of respondents. Rare, for example, is the survey that does not present the data separately for different racial or sex groups. Consequently, the survey is rare that aims solely to describe *the* public opinion on some issue. Most surveys try, instead, to describe the opinions of different subgroups within the American public because it is believed that information about significant sources of heterogeneity is worth having. Among other things, it can help locate those who support, oppose, or are indifferent toward past or planned actions.

Marketing concepts, the notion of interest group politics, and the growing display of poll data in the media that are broken down by subgroups probably all contribute to a possible shift in public consciousness. Instead of thinking about the American public and the sources of consensus that hold it together, we think more and more about different publics within America and the sources of division that drive them apart. These can be divisions of life style (as in marketing), of interest (as in interest group politics), or of other kinds of preference. When the topic is tax-based support for a variety of welfare groups it is important to test the extent to which there is a homogeneous public opinion, for it is presumably easier to implement tax-related policies where a strong consensus exists than where there are significant divisions.

It is easy to imagine that the American public will be divided in its support for welfare groups. The simplest concept of self-interest predicts this, for it may well be that groups categorized in a certain way (e.g., persons with poverty-level income) are more likely to support tax-funded services for the poor than for other segments of society; or that persons who might easily become members of a certain category should support services for that category (e.g., persons living on the San Andreas earthquake fault might especially favor disaster victims; or persons nearing retirement might especially prefer services for the elderly). Self-interest is not, of course, the only variable that may lead to different kinds of persons preferring different welfare groups over others. Other possible explanatory variables include: knowing people in particular welfare groups; differences in the level of need that one attributes to each group; or differences in whether or not the plight of the person in need is self-caused.

A second reason exists for expecting that the public may be heterogeneous in its support of tax-based services for welfare groups. In Chapter 3 we saw that the Chicago public

at large "used" a differentiated cognitive structure in determining support. Decisions were made not solely in terms of
groups or services but in terms of the fit between groups and
services. Consequently, the rank ordering of preferences
among the groups differed from service to service. Intuitively,
it would not seem reasonable to expect different segments of
the public to have the same cognitive structure as the population as a whole. Although we might perhaps expect that
different racial, sex, income, or occupational groups might
consistently prefer one group—say, the disabled elderly—it is
not easy to expect (1) that for any one service, these subgroups would give similar patterns of support to the disabled
elderly *and six other* welfare groups; and (2) that for some
other service, there would be a different pattern of support,
but one that was shared by all the subgroups. If we found
consistency of preferences that shifted from service to service
in the same way for each subgroup of respondents, this
would suggest (but not necessarily "prove") that the respondents shared similar information environments which had
shaped their preferences as to who should be supported most
or least. Can we expect such a homogeneity of environment
for, say, poor elderly minority group members and affluent
young whites when their tastes, political interests, and
sources of information would appear to differ so radically?

The problem addressed in this chapter is: How much
homogeneity is there in the way that different groups within
the Chicago public determine their pattern of tax-based support for welfare groups? A high degree of homogeneity
would suggest that political action based on support preferences would be all the easier, whereas a high degree of
heterogeneity would suggest great political difficulties in
using public opinion to codetermine any actions. For a number of reasons—largely relating to differences in self-interest
and information environments—we would not expect much
homogeneity in the preferences of different groups. But since
the issue has not been explored in prior survey research in

any detail, it is an open issue. Fortunately, it is also an issue open to empirical test.

Problems in Examining the Homogeneity Issue

It is not easy to probe issues of homogeneity among population subgroups. There are many reasons for this. First, it is not always clear whether one is looking for respondent group differences in the *ordering* of preferences among the welfare groups as opposed to, say, respondent differences in the mean *level* of support for groups. It is possible, for example, to imagine high- , middle- , and low-income groups giving the same rank order as to who should be supported, but *one* income group giving consistently higher levels of support to all the welfare groups. For any one service, is it the order of preference among welfare groups or the level of preference for each group that is more meaningful for inferring the degree of homogeneity among population subgroups?

When it is clear that policy-makers or the general public may be forced to make choices among a specific set of welfare groups, a case can be made that rank orderings are more important than mean levels of support. In fact, the case was made in Chapter 1 that these welfare groups are already in competition for finite resources which are likely to decrease in the future in real terms. Since the political conflict is likely to be posed in terms of which group is more supported for which service, it would seem particularly useful to know how widely shared among the general public is a particular ordinal ranking. Then one could draw conclusions of the type: blacks and whites share the same preferences, or blacks prefer the poor over the disabled, whereas whites have the opposite preference. Such statements could be made irrespective of whether blacks give more support than whites for all welfare groups.

The difficulty with such an argument is that a rank ordering is extremely dependent on the particular welfare groups
being compared. If one were to change the groups, it is
possible that the rank orderings would change. Moreover,
they might conceivably change in different ways for different
respondent groups. This possibility has to inspire the modest
realization that, in our research, no empirical findings about
the degree of homogeneity in rankings can be generalized
beyond the seven groups being compared. Generalization is
also limited when we compare the mean level of support
offered to a particular welfare group by one respondent
group as opposed to another. This is because means are
presumably also sensitive to the context in which the measurement is made. But our belief is that mean levels of
support will be somewhat more stable than rankings when a
change is made in the other welfare groups being compared.
This should be especially true in the experiment where respondents do not make any direct comparisons among specifically labeled welfare groups but rather decide their support level on the basis of each individual vignette character's
condition and situation. In any event, though we favor de-
fining homogeneity in terms of ranks, we shall also present
and discuss data about mean levels of support. And we shall
do this for the nonexperimental and experimental sections of
the survey.

A second problem in assessing homogeneity concerns the
context of comparison. We speculated above that both rank
orderings and mean levels of support might be affected by
the welfare groups being compared. Similarly, it is possible
that the order or level of support might be affected differently for different respondent groups if they were asked
about their willingness to support particular welfare groups in
comparison to nonwelfare issues—say, nuclear reactors,
greater defense spending, or pollution control. Circumventing
this problem would require more resources than we had
available, and so we want to stress that the results presented

in this chapter cannot be generalized beyond a context where Chicago–area residents rated seven welfare groups (out of the many that could be rated) for a small set of social services (out of many with a claim on the public purse), and that no comparisons were offered with nonwelfare claims on the public purse.

A third problem in determining the degree of homogeneity lies in the statistical criteria one chooses for concluding that the profile of support for welfare groups is similar or different from one respondent group to another. In the survey part of the research to be presented, we conducted two analyses. First, we correlated the rank orderings of support for the seven welfare groups across particular respondent groups (e.g., blacks and whites). Second, we tested the resulting rank correlations for statistical significance. Third, we conducted conventional t-tests between the mean support levels offered by one respondent group when compared to another. In the experimental section of the study, an analysis of variance was performed. Main effects of respondent groups would suggest that the groups being compared differed in the support they reportedly wanted to give, and statistically significant interactions between respondent and vignette characteristics would suggest that respondent groups differed in how they allocated their support across welfare groups. On the other hand, if there were no such interactions, this would imply that different kinds of respondent groups had similar support patterns.

A fourth problem in determining homogeneity lies in the selection of the respondent groups whose similarity or difference in support judgments is to be assessed. The researcher cannot hope to break down the data by all possible respondent categories because there would be too few respondents in each category to draw meaningful conclusions. As outlined in Chapter 2, we employed a sampling design which allowed us to distinguish among 24 total subsets of the population based on a mix of the criteria of race, sex, age, and income.

This means we could compare many subgroups, but obviously not all that might be relevant. However, the ones we could examine are important. Since the welfare groups differed in poverty and age, breaking the data down by the income level and age of respondents permits us to learn if self-interest might be influencing the support preferences of low-income and poorer respondents. Breaking down the data by race and sex also makes sense since race is consistently related to beliefs about high levels of tax support for groups in need and little is known about whether the sexes differ in their support for particular welfare groups.

LEVELS AND PATTERNS OF SUPPORT AMONG POPULATION SUBGROUPS

Race

One of the survey questions is about the extent to which respondents think that social services should be increased or reduced for each of the seven welfare groups. Blacks and whites differ consistently on this general support question, with blacks being more likely than whites to support an overall increase in services for each of the seven groups ($p < .001$).

However, though the *magnitude* of black support is greater for each group, the *order* is very similar to that of the whites. This similarity is clear in Table 4.1, where it can be seen that the correlation (Spearman's Rho) between the ranking of blacks and whites is .93 ($p < .01$) for general services. Each race group gives the most support to disabled children and the disabled elderly and the least support to the poor under 65.

For each of the four service programs, respondents had 20 $5,000 bills to distribute across seven groups. Since most

Table 4.1 : Support for General Services Examined by Race of
Respondent[a]

	Mean Support by Race		Spearman's Rho[b]
Welfare Group	Blacks	Whites	
(1) Disabled children	6.59 (1)	5.52 (2)***	
(2) Disabled elderly	6.49 (2)	5.55 (1)***	
(3) Disabled adults under 65	6.44 (3)	5.31 (4)***	.93
(4) Poor elderly	6.26 (4)	5.33 (3)***	(p < .01)
(5) Poor children	6.16 (5)	4.91 (6)***	
(6) Disaster victims	6.07 (6)	5.17 (5)***	
(7) Poor adults under 65	5.74 (7)	4.45 (7)***	

a. Three asterisks represent a difference between blacks' and whites' support
means of p < .001; two asterisks, p < .01; one asterisk, p < .05.
b. This is a correlation coefficient with upper bound equal to +1 and lower
bound equal to −1 (see Conover, 1971: 245-249).

respondents allocated the same total of funds—$100,000—the
scale is ipsative, and when the mean for any one welfare
group is high the mean for some other group has to be low.
Therefore, we cannot say that blacks or whites give a different *overall* level of support (for each, it is a total of
$100,000); rather, we can examine (1) which welfare groups
are preferred most by each racial group and (2) the similarity
between each race in its preference ranking among welfare
groups.

Considering the first issue of which groups are preferred
most by each race, we see in Table 4.2 that for nutrition
programs, whites prefer to help the disabled elderly more
than do blacks, that and blacks prefer to help disabled adults
under 65 and especially disabled children and poor adults
under 65. As for transportation, the only reliable race differences are for supporting poor children and adults under 65,
where blacks give more aid. With education programs, the
only difference is a greater preference by blacks for helping
poor children. The data for a guaranteed income policy are
harder to interpret since this was the only item where blacks

Table 4.2: Support for Specific Services Examined by Race of Respondent

Welfare Group	Mean Support by Race		Spearman's Rho[a]
	Blacks	Whites	
Nutrition Programs			
(1) Poor elderly	$15,700 (1)	$16,100 (2)	
(2) Disabled elderly	15,650 (2)	17,850 (1)**	
(3) Disabled adults under 65	14,850 (3)	13,650 (3)*	.79
(4) Poor children	13,750 (4)	13,200 (4)	(p < .05)
(5) Disabled children	13,750 (5)	10,850 (6)***	
(6) Poor adults under 65	12,600 (6)	9,550 (7)***	
(7) Disaster victims	11,050 (7)	12,650 (5)	
Transportation Programs			
(1) Disabled children	$15,900 (1)	$16,050 (1)	
(2) Disabled elderly	15,900 (2)	15,900 (2)	
(3) Disabled adults under 65	15,050 (3)	14,950 (3)	.89
(4) Poor children	14,400 (4)	10,100 (6)***	(p < .01)
(5) Poor elderly	14,200 (5)	13,400 (4)	
(6) Disaster victims	11,350 (6)	10,950 (5)	
(7) Poor adults under 65	11,300 (7)	8,600 (7)***	
Guaranteed Minimum Income Programs			
(1) Disabled elderly	$16,300 (1)	$15,900 (1)	
(2) Disabled adults under 65	15,100 (2)	12,900 (4)***	
(3) Poor elderly	15,050 (3)	13,050 (2)***	.89
(4) Disabled children	14,250 (4)	12,950 (3)	(p < .01)
(5) Poor children	13,750 (5)	10,200 (5)***	
(6) Poor adults under 65	12,550 (6)	8,350 (6)***	
(7) Disaster victims	10,000 (7)	8,200 (7)**	
Education Programs			
(1) Poor adults under 65	$16,750 (1)	$16,150 (1)	
(2) Disabled adults under 65	15,650 (2)	15,850 (2)	
(3) Poor children	15,000 (3)	11,400 (6)***	.79
(4) Disabled children	14,950 (4)	15,550 (3)	(p < .05)
(5) Disabled elderly	13,350 (5)	12,850 (4)	
(6) Poor elderly	12,700 (6)	12,300 (5)	
(7) Disaster victims	10,150 (7)	9,350 (7)	

a. See note b in Table 4.1.

and whites differed in their willingness to spend all the simulated money assigned to them. As many as 27 percent of the whites refused to distribute everything as compared to only 7 percent of the blacks. The guaranteed income question aside, the rest of the data suggest that blacks are more disposed than whites to help the poor and adults of working age.

But the more striking feature of Table 4.2 is the consistency in rank orderings between blacks and whites across all of the services studied. The Spearman Rho values are all .79 or above and are all different from zero to a statistically significant degree despite the low number of ranks and the corresponding low power of the test. These correlations indicate that blacks and whites are homogeneous in their support preferences, *even as these preferences shift from service to service*. Where there are differences—and these are of minor magnitude when compared to the similarities—this is because blacks prefer to help poor persons and persons of working age whereas whites place a slightly greater emphasis on the disabled and elderly.

Income

Table 4.3 gives the results when respondents are classified into three income groups and the general services question is examined that is not ipsative. Here it can be seen that the income groups differ to a statistically reliable degree in their mean support for only two groups: poor children and poor adults under 65. In each case, most support is offered by low-income respondents, and the middle- and high-income respondents do not differ. The same pattern is observable for the only group where differences were marginally reliable ($p < .10$), and this was for the other poor group: the elderly poor.

An assessment of the similarity between respondent groups in their rank-order preferences among the welfare groups is

Table 4.3:   Support for General Services Examined by Income of
             Respondent

| | | Support by Income Groups | | | Friedman's |
	Welfare Group	Low	Middle	High	T^a
(1)	Disabled elderly	6.17 (1)	6.01 (2)	5.86 (2)	
(2)	Disabled children	6.12 (2)	6.05 (1)	5.98 (1)	
(3)	Disabled adults				
	under 65	6.04 (3)	5.76 (3)	5.81 (3)	17.71
(4)	Poor elderly	5.98 (4)	5.69 (4)	5.70 (4)	$(p < .01)$
(5)	Disaster victims	5.78 (5)	5.50 (5)	5.59 (5)	
(6)	Poor children	5.75 (6)	5.45 (6)	5.38 (6)*	
(7)	Poor adults under				
	65	5.43 (7)	4.89 (7)	4.95 (7)**	

a. The Friedman Test Statistic is distributed like chi-square. Here it has six
degrees of freedom (see Conover, 1971: 265-269).

offered by Friedman's test statistic. This shows that, even
with the low power of the test in question, the groups'
rankings are similar. Indeed, inspection of the actual ranks—
reported in parentheses in Table 4.3—shows an almost perfect
correspondence of rankings of the welfare groups in all three
of the income groups.

If we turn now to the specific programs, and because of
the ipsative nature of the scale consider only the correspondence in ranks, Table 4.4 tells the same story as Table 4.3
did in terms of an increase in general services. Irrespective of
whether nutrition, transportation, guaranteed income, or
education services are involved, the three different income
groups have very similar preference orderings. What is so
striking about this is that the preference ordering differs from
service to service; so that the similarity in preference rankings
among income groups does not reflect a "knee-jerk" preference for some groups over others. The discernment we noted
in Chapter 3 when considering the Chicago public at large is
matched in both racial and income groups, all of whom make
the same discerning choices.

Table 4.4: Support for Specific Services by Income of Respondent

Welfare Groups	Mean Support by Income			Friedman's T[a]
	Low	Middle	High	
Nutrition Programs				
(1) Disabled elderly	$15,900 (1)	$17,650 (1)	$16,600 (1)	
(2) Poor elderly	15,450 (2)	15,900 (2)	16,350 (2)	
(3) Disabled adults under 65	13,500 (3)	14,600 (3)	14,550 (3)	17.71
(4) Poor children	13,200 (4)	12,560 (5)	14,200 (4)	(p < .01)
(5) Disabled children	12,450 (5)	12,800 (4)	11,650 (5)	
(6) Disaster victims	12,350 (6)	12,050 (6)	11,150 (6)	
(7) Poor adults under 65	11,950 (7)	10,850 (7)	10,500 (7)	
Transportation Programs				
(1) Disabled children	$15,650 (1)	$16,400 (2)	$16,050 (1)	
(2) Disabled elderly	15,350 (2)	16,500 (1)	15,850 (2)	
(3) Disabled adults under 65	14,600 (3)	15,500 (3)	14,850 (3)	17.71
(4) Poor elderly	13,800 (4)	14,350 (4)	13,350 (4)	(p < .01)
(5) Poor children	12,300 (5)	11,750 (5)	12,700 (5)	
(6) Disaster victims	12,250 (6)	10,850 (6)	10,350 (6)	
(7) Poor adults under 65	10,050 (7)	9,950 (7)	9,900 (7)	

Table 4.4: Support for Specific Services by Income of Respondent (Cont)

Welfare Groups	Mean Support by Income			Friedman's T[a]
	Low	Middle	High	
Guaranteed Minimum Income Programs				
(1) Disabled elderly	$16,250 (1)	$16,550 (1)	$15,400 (1)	
(2) Poor elderly	14,100 (2)	14,400 (3)	13,700 (3)	
(3) Disabled children	12,900 (3)	15,000 (2)	12,900 (4)*	16.67
(4) Poor children	11,950 (4)	11,950 (5)	12,100 (5)	(p < .05)
(5) Disabled adults under 65	11,500 (5)	13,900 (4)	14,100 (2)	
(6) Poor adults under 65	11,050 (6)	9,350 (6-7)	11,000 (6)	
(7) Disaster victims	9,700 (7)	9,350 (6-7)	8,300 (7)	
Education Programs				
(1) Poor adults under 65	$16,200 (1)	$15,700 (3)	$16,700 (1)	
(2) Disabled adults under 65	15,500 (2)	15,800 (2)	15,950 (2)	
(3) Disabled children	14,600 (3)	16,950 (1)	14,200 (4)**	15.92
(4) Disabled elderly	13,800 (4)	13,350 (4)	12,150 (5)	(p < .05)
(5) Poor elderly	12,800 (5)	12,750 (6)	12,000 (6)	
(6) Poor children	12,350 (6)	12,800 (5)	14,450 (3)*	
(7) Disaster victims	9,800 (7)	9,300 (7)	9,300 (7)	

a. See note a, Table 4.3.

Age

The age group to which respondents belong appears to have no relationship to their level of support for an increase in general services. Nor does it have any relationship to the pattern of support for three of the particular programs we examined. Thus, the respondents' age does not, in general, affect their ratings. The same discerning preferences are made at all ages.

However, there is one exception to this general trend. A main effect of age *is* found in support for education programs. Respondents over 50 are significantly more likely than respondents under 50 to assign more funds to education programs for the elderly poor, the elderly disabled, and disaster victims ($p < .05$ in each case). The reverse relationship between age and support occurred for education programs for poor children and poor adults under 65. Adults 50 and over are least likely to support these groups for education services, while younger adults are most likely to support them. When the age groups are trichotomized into 21-22, 45-64, and 65 and over, the same relationship holds with the 45-64 age groups always having support levels somewhere in between the youngest and oldest age groups.

Discussion of the relationship between both age and race and the willingness to support an increase in general social services must be qualified because of significant interactions

Table 4.5: **Amount Distributed for Education Programs by Respondents in Three Age Groups**

Age of R[a]	Elderly Disabled	Elderly Poor	Disaster Victims	Poor Under 65	Poor Children
21–44	$12,100	$11,900	$ 8,950	$17,450	$14,350
45–64	13,650	12,800	10,150	15,500	12,800
65 and over	14,200	13,250	10,750	14,750	11,350

a. "R" means respondent group.

(all p values < .01) between race and age on the question
about support for disabled children, disabled elderly persons,
poor children, and poor elderly persons. The interaction
means are presented in Table 4.6.

Consider first black responses to support for the disabled.
It can be seen that support for the disabled—both elderly and
children—is high and that although the variation in black
support is not large, persons over 50 are somewhat more
supportive than persons under 50. However, among whites,
age makes more of a difference, and whites under 50 are
significantly more supportive of disabled children and disabled elderly persons than are whites over 50.

Similar race-age interactions are found on the same measure of support for increased services for poor children and
elderly poor. Whites over 50 are significantly less likely to
support services for poor children and elderly persons than
whites under 50, while blacks over 50 are significantly *more*
likely to support services for these groups of poor than are
blacks under 50.

Sex

No statistically significant main effects of sex could be
found for the question about a general increase in the level of

Table 4.6: Race and Age Differences in Support for an Overall
Increase in Services for Disabled and Poor Children
and Elderly Persons

| | Disabled | | | | Poor | | | |
| | Elderly | | Children | | Elderly | | Children | |
Age of R[a]	Black Rs	White Rs	Black Rs	White Rs	Black Rs	White Rs	Black Rs	White Rs
Under 50 Rs	6.42	5.82	6.52	5.74	6.13	5.58	5.96	5.09
Over 50 Rs	6.55	5.26	6.67	5.28	6.40	5.06	6.39	4.72

a. "R" means respondent group.

support. However, for all four of the specific programs for poor and disabled children, significant race by sex interaction patterns are obtained. The consistent pattern is that *white females* are significantly more likely than white males to support programs for both poor and disabled children. There is less variation among blacks, but the trend is clearly the reverse from the white pattern: *Black males* tended to be more supportive than black females (see Table 4.7). The race-sex interactions are specific to services for children insofar as no such interactions were obtained for services for persons under 65 or for the elderly. Again, we must remember that these differences are in respect to *levels* of support. *Patterns* are the same.

Education

When respondents consider whether there should be a general increase in services for the seven groups, the education level of respondents is significantly related to support. The relationship is monotonic and negative, with respondents who have less than high school education being the most supportive; high school graduates being somewhat less supportive; people with some college education being still less supportive; and college graduates being the least supportive ($p < .05$ for every welfare group, but elderly poor where $p < .10$). Though the level of support is different, the patterns of support are similar.

Education ceases to have any relationship to support when respondents consider how they as "policy-makers" would distribute $100,000 in resources to individual education, transportation, nutrition, and income programs. For most of the programs, there is little difference among the four educational groups as to how they would distribute funds. Thus, it appears that the education groups differ in the magnitude of their support levels when services are considered in the *gen-*

Table 4.7: Race by Sex Interactions in Support for Programs for Children

Support for Nutrition Programs for

Sex	Poor Children		Disabled Children	
	Black R[a]	White R	Black R	White R
Male R	$14,450	$10,450	$14,350	$ 9,950
Female R	14,200	12,300	13,100	11,750

Support for Income Programs for

	Poor Children		Disabled Children	
	Black R	White R	Black R	White R
Male R	$14,750	$ 9,100	$14,500	$12,250
Female R	12,850	11,350	14,050	13,550

Support for Education Programs for

	Poor Children		Disabled Children	
	Black R	White R	Black R	White R
Male R	$15,800	$10,450	$15,200	$14,200
Female R	14,200	12,300	14,750	17,000

Support for Transportation Programs for

	Poor Children		Disabled Children	
	Black R	White R	Black R	White R
Male R	$14,700	$ 8,750	$16,300	$13,600
Female R	14,150	11,400	15,400	16,350

a. "R" means respondent group.

eralized abstract sense; but when *particular* services are described, there is little difference among educational groups.

Only for education services is there any pattern of significant interactions among people at different educational levels. College educated people are the least likely to support educational services for the disabled elderly ($p < .01$), for the elderly poor ($p < .05$), and for disaster victims ($p < .05$). However, the relationship changes and is monotonic in the opposite direction for education programs for *poor children*. Here, college graduates are the most supportive, and persons who have not graduated from high school are the least supportive. When the relationship between education and programs for poor children is examined among blacks and whites, the relationship is seen to be dramatically stronger among blacks than among whites. At the different educational levels, especially the first three, whites do not differ very much from each other. Blacks, on the other hand, grow more supportive with each increase in level of education (see Table 4.8).

Findings from the Nutrition Scale

The foregoing analyses suggest: (1) a striking similarity between race, sex, age, income, and education groups in how they rank the seven welfare groups we studied for four services and for an increase in general services; (2) a prefer-

Table 4.8: **Education and Race Differences in Resource Distribution to Education Programs for Poor Children**

Education	White Rs[a]	N	Black Rs	N
Less than high school	$11,300	(47)	$13,250	(83)
High school graduates	11,100	(50)	14,350	(38)
Some college	11,200	(45)	16,350	(45)
College graduates	11,950	(49)	19,800	(23)

a. "R" means respondent group.

ence by blacks and lower-income persons to give more overall support than whites or middle- and higher-income persons, whereas age and sex groups do not differ in the willingness to give help in any simple way; (3) in the small number of instances where there are differences between respondent groups in their support for particular welfare groups, these differences are usually such that blacks and poorer groups show a relatively stronger preference for the poor and adults under 65, whereas whites and more affluent groups show a relatively stronger preference for the disabled and the elderly. We want now to investigate whether these same patterns hold when we analyze the results from the nutrition questions that were answered using a nonipsative scale heavily weighted toward a reported willingness to pay more taxes.

The results from the action-oriented nutrition support measure are in Table 4.9. Blacks are more willing to offer support than whites for all seven welfare groups. This is by far the strongest relationship in the data, and it is particularly instructive to note that blacks and whites differ most of all in their support for poor adults under 65. However, as is true with the other measures of support, the overall support patterns of blacks and whites are similar at a statistically significant level.

Table 4.9: Support for Nutrition Services on the Action Scale by Race of Respondents

| Welfare Group | Mean Support by Race | | Spearman's Rho |
	Blacks	Whites	
Disabled elderly	16.84 (1)	15.03 (1)	
Poor elderly	16.75 (2)	14.45 (2)	
Disabled adults under 65	16.51 (3)	14.38 (3)	
Poor adults under 65	15.29 (4)	10.09 (7)	.79 (p < .05)
Disaster victims	14.97 (5)	13.06 (4)	
Poor children	14.76 (6)	12.59 (5)	
Disabled children	14.08 (7)	10.42 (6)	

Table 4.10:   Support for Nutrition Services on the Action Scale by
              Income of Respondents

Welfare Group	Mean Support by Income			Friedman's T
	High	Middle	Low	
(1) Disabled elderly	15.82 (1)	16.35 (1)	15.68 (2)	
(2) Poor elderly	15.79 (2)	16.03 (2)	15.89 (1)	
(3) Disabled under 65	15.48 (3)	15.59 (3)	15.47 (3)	
(4) Disaster victims	13.44 (4)	14.30 (4)	14.32 (4)*	17.32
(5) Poor children	13.39 (5)	13.39 (5)	14.23 (5)*	(p < .01)
(6) Poor adults under 65	11.91 (6)	12.23 (7)	13.91 (6)**	
(7) Disabled children	11.42 (7)	12.56 (6)	12.74 (7)*	

As far as income is concerned, the three income groups have almost identical patterns of distributing their support among the seven welfare groups. However, the levels of support they are willing to give differ for poor adults under 65, poor children, and disabled children. In each case, lower income groups offer more support (see Table 4.10).

For six of the seven welfare groups, neither age nor sex is related in any consistent way to the level of support offered for nutrition services. The only exception is support for one group—poor adults under 65, where the young are more supportive than the old on both the summary support index and all the separate items.

VIGNETTE RESULTS

The experiment affords an opportunity to learn if the nonexperimental survey results can be replicated using different methodology: Rather than asking respondents about a group—say, disabled adults under 65—we describe a disabled adult under 65 in a vignette. How are the race, sex, age, and income of respondents related to the support they give to individuals portrayed in vignettes?

The same two questions are addressed in the experiment as in the survey. The first is: Do respondents of different race, sex, age, and income offer different *levels* of support to vignette characters? The second question is: Do respondents have different *patterns* of preferences for vignette characters—e.g., do blacks and whites respond differently to the experimental manipulation of, say, disability or poverty? The question about levels of support can be examined by looking to the main effect of race, sex, age, and income. (Note: Main effects can be examined since the scale used to measure support is not ipsative, i.e., there is no set limit on support so that giving support to one group does not leave less support for other groups.) The question about patterns of preference can be examined by looking to the statistical interaction of respondent and vignette characteristics. In all the results to be presented, the support measure is the behaviorally weighted index; and Hays ω^2 = .01 (see Chapter 2) is the cutting point for inferring significant differences.

Levels of Support

The analysis of variance shows that blacks offer more support to vignette characters overall than do whites. The respective means are 63.02 and 39.84, and this accounts for about 14 percent of the support variance that can be accounted for. This, it will be remembered, is the same relationship that is obtained in the survey with the general support measure.

The analysis also shows that men volunteer higher levels of support than women. The means are 53.67 and 49.20 respectively, and this difference accounts for about 1 percent of the variance. However, the sex effects have to be interpreted in the context of a significant interaction between race and sex (ω^2 = .01). Among whites, males and females do not differ (means = 40.26 and 39.40); but among blacks, men give considerably more help than women (means = 67.05 and 58.99). Somewhat similar findings emerge in the traditional survey section, where black males are more supportive than black females for four programs for poor and disabled children. However, white females tend to be more supportive than white males for these same programs, which is not the case in the experiment.

The income level of respondents is linearly and negatively related to support, and accounts for about 1 percent of the variance. The means are low income, 54.48, moderate income, 52.55; and high income, 47.24. This is also the relationship observed in the survey question about support for an increase in social services.

Age is not related to support in any simple way in the experiment, just as it is not in the survey except for education programs. However, age and race do interact in the experiment. Whites over 50 are less supportive than whites under 50 (means = 37.13 and 42.55, respectively), but blacks over 50 are more supportive than blacks under 50 (mean = 64.94 versus 61.11). Once again, these relationships are like those in the survey.

Patterns of Support

Do respondent groups differ in how they react to the poverty, disability, and age of the vignette characters? The answer to this is "probably not in any significant way." Though ten interactions involving respondent and vignette characteristics attained the 5 percent level of significance (without adjustment for the large number of comparisons made), the largest of them accounts for no more than 1/2 percent of the variance in the support index. Consequently, we do not attribute much weight to such interactions, and we conclude that men and women, blacks and whites, young and old, and persons at all income levels responded to the particular vignette characteristics studied in approximately similar fashion.

In other words, the Chicago public is, in general, homogeneous in how it uses the characteristics of poverty, disability, and age in determining which of the groups should get more support. Respondents differed in the level of support offered, but not in judgments about who should get more support among the welfare groups we studied. This was also the case in the traditional part of the survey, to which the experimental part adds the power of replication plus one finding not considered in the survey. This is that by our criterion of $\omega^2 = 1$, the Chicago public is homogeneous in how it responds to the difference between acute and chronic disability and poverty.

SUMMARY

The evidence reviewed in this chapter suggests that some respondent groups differ in their *level of support* for social welfare groups but not in their *patterns of support* for these groups. Concerning levels of support, blacks offer more support than whites and lower-income persons more than higher-income persons. Though age groups do not differ in their willingness to help in general, an exception is that the elderly are more supportive of education programs for the elderly than are younger persons. Also, whites under 50 are more supportive of programs for disabled children and disabled elderly than are whites over 50. This pattern is just the reverse among blacks over 50 and under 50. Males and females differ not at all in levels of support until the data are broken down by race. Then we see that black males tend to be more supportive than black females; whereas if there is any difference at all among whites, it is likely to be in the opposite direction.

These few differences between respondent groups in how they reacted to the plight of specific welfare groups pale beside the consistent evidence which indicates highly similar rank-order preferences from all of the respondent groups for each social service. Time and again, the data analyses suggest that the same relative preferences were held by all of the segments of the Chicago public that were studied. There does seem, then, to be a homogeneous public that differs in how much support should be given but not in who should receive the support.

The homogeneity of the public is not due to a reflexive stereotypical preference for some groups applied willy-nilly to all services. We saw in Chapter 3 that the Chicago public is discerning in its support, with different groups favored for different services. The homogeneity of the public is best seen within the context of such discernment, for the similarity of support profiles across respondent groups is a differently ordered similarity from service to service. This means that the Chicago public is homogeneous *and* discerning, presumably because cues about social dependency are encoded and evaluated in similar ways by rich and poor, black and white, male and female, young and old.

The present findings about homogeneous discernment should not be overgeneralized. Clearly, they are limited to Chicago, to quota samples with unknown (but probably small) biases, to comparisons involving seven particular welfare groups when others could have been selected, and to comparisons where no alternatives outside of the welfare domain were made salient. Moreover, some small differences between respondent groups were obtained, most of which suggested that in the rare cases where respondent groups differed in their support for particular welfare groups, this was in the direction of greater support for groups of which one was, or soon might be, a member.

CONCLUSION

Notions from marketing research of segmentation and from political science of interest group politics would have led one to expect that the public is divided in its support for welfare groups. Analysts of political behavior tell us of "conflicting forces" within the public that are not "easily reconciled" (Nie et al., 1976: 2). An understanding of self-interest would suggest that persons in a certain category (for example, the poor) would be more likely to support services for that social welfare category than would other segments of society. However, the survey results do not reveal the heterogeneity among the public that might have been expected. On the contrary, the patterns of support differ in relatively minor ways among racial, income, age, or sex subgroups. With respect to *level* of support, however, differences exist. Though blacks and whites share the same preference, blacks offer more support than whites, especially if they are males over 50 and of low income. Whites are less supportive in general, though younger and low-income whites are more supportive than upper-income whites. These findings are true in both the experimental and nonexperimental sections of the survey.

To understand the importance of the similar patterns of support among diverse respondent subgroups, it is useful to see this homogeneity against a broader backdrop. The 1960s and 1970s have been periods of growing divisions within the American electorate (Nie et al., 1976). Politics has become increasingly group based, and the argument is often made that the politician tries as much as possible to use this divisiveness as a working guide to what he or she must do to win elections. "From the stump . . . politicians righteously deplore any suggestion that their red-blooded constituents might be influenced by bloc-voting patterns; off the stump they find it hard to discuss strategy in any other terms" (quoted by Nie et al., 1976: 213). On many issues, politicians are correct in expecting various subgroups to hold different opinions. That is why the homogeneity among the public on preference patterns for welfare groups is important. Here is one area where there appears to be consensus.

What makes this consensus all the more impressive is that it is not of the simple kind, e.g., the disabled elderly being preferred to poor adults under 65. It is much more complex and contingent: The disabled elderly are preferred to poor adults under 65 for some services but not for other services. The similar rank ordering of preferences shifts from service to service in the same way for each welfare group. This consistency in similar but different orderings of preferences is repeated across five service questions and thus strengthens the argument that the public is not only discerning but also *homogeneously* discerning.

Of course, all subgroups do not give the same level of support. In interpreting the degree of homogeneity among population subgroups, we believe the order of preference may be more important than the level. Resources are finite, and the political decision must be how they are distributed among subgroups. An illustration of this can be seen in allocation of Title XX social service funds. Although federal guidelines mandate that recipients of public assistance (SSI, AFDC, and Medicaid) get a certain number of services which have specific goals, states have a wide margin of discretion in deciding exactly how Title XX resources should be distributed among groups. State planners, service providers, and consumer groups are all competing for their welfare group's slice of the service pie, according to many analysts (Gilbert, 1977: 39). Though there may be competition at this level, the findings of the survey reported here reveal agreement among diverse segments of the respondents about the order in which resources should be distributed.

What are the implications of the public being so homogeneous in their judgments of support preferences? First, the homogeneity implies that policy-making can be done with a greater understanding of what the public will sanction. Politi-

cal action is easier if it acts upon a public opinion that is
unified rather than one that is segmented. Without knowledge, policy-makers make decisions based on what they *think*
public opinion is. Political leaders may react to *perceived*
public preferences that one group get priority treatment
regardless of the social service in question. This response
would have unfortunate consequences for other welfare
groups who may be left out of the distribution process.
Though it is the case that the disabled and the elderly are
often preferred, this is not always true. As is pointed out in
Chapter 3, the link between the group and the service is
evident. Program planners who are able to establish a direct
linkage between the need of the group and the service, may
find a homogeneous public support behind their efforts.

A second implication of this homogeneity points to a
public with a common ideology shaping its preferences as to
what kinds of people should be supported most or least.
What this ideology might be can be explored by trying to
understand what causes the differentiation in support. An
attempt to understand reasons for support differences is the
aim of Chapter 5.

TOWARD AN EXPLANATION OF

DIFFERENCES IN SUPPORT

This chapter reports the results of analyses designed to probe why some groups are supported more than others. As in previous chapters, the discussion will be in two parts: one concerned with the traditional survey part of the study and the other with the experimental part. It is generally acknowledged that experiments are superior to surveys for testing causal hypotheses. But since experiments permit assessing the effects of fewer potential causes, they are more warranted after traditional surveys have been conducted to probe causal relationships and reduce the list of causal contenders. To conduct an experiment simultaneously with a survey implies knowing in advance which are the most important potential causes. We did not know this. However, the two had to be carried out at the same time in this research project, and we were forced to select our independent variables—not from the results of a prior survey—but from a review of research and theoretical literature, including the speculation of experts, survey findings, and prior experiments on helping, most of which were conducted in laboratory settings. We have no guarantee that the variables selected from such a review are the most important ones, and we may have omitted from consideration some variables that do indeed explain why some groups are helped more than others.

In probing the traditional survey data, we shall report the results of two new analyses. The first uses as the criterion of support the standardized index derived from the four measures which required respondents to distribute play money and from the increase in services scale. For reasons that will soon become clear, the first analysis will be called the "pattern-matching analysis." The second analysis is more extensive, dealing with more support measures and a wider range of potential explanatory variables than the pattern-matching analysis. The second analysis, for reasons that should again become clear later, will be called "the difference score analysis."

THE PATTERN-MATCHING ANALYSIS

Intuitively, we would expect any variable that explains the support index to be distributed like the support measure. That is, we would expect the social welfare group that receives most support to score highest on a valid explanatory variable; and we would expect the least helped group to score lowest on a valid explanatory variable. What needs explaining, then, is the pattern of mean support scores across the seven welfare groups; and to be a contender as an explanatory variable, the pattern of means for that variable has to match the pattern of the support means. If the patterns do not match, it would seem that the variable in question does not explain why people support the groups they do. If there is a close match, it would seem that the variable might explain why people support the groups they do.

Figure 5.1a displays the pattern to be matched. It can be seen that the mean support for disabled groups is higher than for poor groups, that support for disabled persons increases slightly with age, and that the poor elderly and poor children are helped more than poor adults. Disaster victims are helped least.

Figure 5.1b shows how the seven groups are rated for *deservingness*. The data seem similar to the support data, except for the mean for disaster victims. Also, the disabled groups are seen as equally deserving, regardless of age.

Figure 5.1c presents the means for *perceived gratefulness*. This, too, resembles the pattern to be matched. Again, the exception is disaster victims, who are rated highest in gratefulness but lowest for support.

Figure 5.1d shows the means for judgments about whether members of a particular welfare group are *responsible for their own fate or not*. Here the pattern of means is different from the support pattern. This difference is due to the fact that among both the disabled and the poor, children are seen as less responsible for their fate than both the elderly and adults, but children do not receive more support than the elderly. Also, disaster victims are seen as least responsible for their fate, but receive lowest support. Though there are these differences, there are similarities for certain relationships. In every comparison between poor and disabled children, adults under 65, and elderly adults, the disabled rank higher than the poor. This is also the support pattern.

Ratings of the *pleasantness* of each welfare group are in Figure 5.1e. The pattern of means among the disabled and disaster victims is not the same as with the pattern to be matched.

Perceived need results are in Figure 5.1f (ratings of disaster victims were omitted from this analysis). The data pattern resembles that of the pattern to be matched except that there is little difference between poor and disabled children.

Figure 5.1g gives means for a measure of *the likelihood that the respondent will suffer from the welfare group's plight*. Here the data do not closely resemble the data on support; however, the low mean of the disaster group victims is particularly noteworthy.

Finally, Figure 5.1h shows group means for the *percentage of respondents knowing someone whose plight is like that of a welfare group member*—e.g., disabled elderly, poor children, and disaster victims. Here the pattern of means is quite different from the support pattern. The small similarity is that the means for the disabled and disaster groups are like those for support. The means for poor groups and the relationship between the poor and the disabled are quite different.

The pattern-matching analysis is crude and relies heavily on visual judgment. Also, it does not deal with each support measure singly, and no account can be taken of potential explanatory variables at the individual level—age, race, sex, income, degree of belief in a just world, and whether the respondent has ever received welfare. Nonetheless, the pattern-matching analysis suggests that some of the potential explanatory variables are not likely to explain the pattern of group support obtained with data from the standardized support index. These variables are: how pleasant the group members are seen to be and whether or not the respondent perceives that he or she is likely to suffer the plight of particular welfare groups. The other variables—to different degrees—produce data whose pattern matches that of the support index. These are: perceived deservingness, gratefulness, and need. The pattern of two other variables is only similar to certain aspects of the support pattern. Locus of responsibility for plight is similar to the support pattern in two ways—similar patterns of differences between the poor and disabled and between poor adults under 65 and over 65. Also, the pattern of means for people knowing a welfare group member is similar in two respects: in the higher means for the disabled over disaster victims and for the poor over disaster victims.

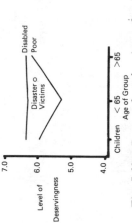

Fig. 5.1a: **Overall support: Relationship of support to age and condition of welfare groups**

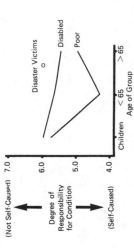

Fig. 5.1b: **Respondents' ratings of welfare groups' level of deservingness**

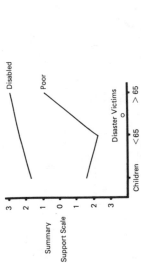

Fig. 5.1c: **Respondents' ratings of welfare groups' level of gratefulness**

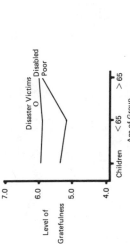

Fig. 5.1d: **Respondents' ratings of extent to which welfare groups' condition is self caused**

131

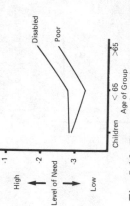

Fig. 5.1e: Respondents' ratings of the pleasantness of welfare groups

Fig. 5.1f: Respondents' ratings of the welfare groups' level of need
(Note: Disaster victims were not rated on this measure)

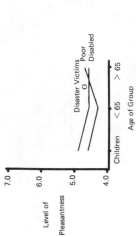

Fig. 5.1g: Respondents' ratings of the likelihood of being in the same condition as a welfare group

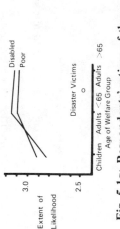

Fig. 5.1h: Percent of respondents who know a member of a welfare group

ANALYSIS OF DIFFERENCE SCORES

A series of analyses will now be presented in which a difference score was computed for each respondent between his or her rating of support for one welfare group and some other group—to be called the comparison group. These support difference scores were then used in multiple regression analyses, where the predictor variables were the differences between the respondents' ratings of the attributes of the same groups with respect to deservingness, need, gratitude, pleasantness, and responsibility for own fate. In addition to these attributes of welfare groups, some psychological and social characteristics of respondents were included in the difference score analysis (age, race, sex, income, years of education, occupational prestige, degree of belief in a just world, likelihood one would become poor or disabled, ever having received government aid, and knowing someone who is poor or disabled).[1] Thus, we compared the differences in support that a respondent gave to any two groups (for example, the poor elderly and poor children) with the difference between these same two groups on a potential explanatory variable (for example, the respondent's perception of the need of the poor elderly and poor children).

We decided that predictor variables which accounted for 1 percent or more of the variance in support differences should remain in consideration as being possibly explanatory, while those that did not could probably be eliminated as explanatory causes. The logic behind this is obvious: an explanatory variable must correlate with what it is thought to explain if it is to be considered explanatory. The 1 percent criterion is less lenient than it seems. The analysis involves predicting difference scores from a set of variables, many of which are also difference scores. Since it includes four sets of measurement error—two per difference score—the analysis cannot result in large relationships.

With seven welfare groups and seven indicators of support (the four money game measures, the general increase in services scale, the nutrition scale, and the summary index), many difference scores can be computed. The first set of analyses to be presented compares age groups within the poor in order to illuminate which variables predict *differences* in support between (1) the poor elderly and poor children, (2) the poor elderly and poor adults under 65; and (3) poor adults under 65 and poor children. The next set of analyses compares age groups within the disabled, giving the same three age comparisons as with the poor. The next analyses compare the poor and disabled within age groups, being comparisons of support between (1) the poor and disabled elderly; (2) poor and disabled persons under 65; and (3) poor and disabled children. The final analyses examine predictors of the difference in the support offered to disaster victims as opposed to the average of adults under 65 and elderly persons who are (1) poor and (2) disabled.

Explaining Differences in Support Between Age Groups

In Chapter 3 we saw that the elderly who are poor receive more support for services than children who are poor, the one exception being for education. Table 5.1 shows that the poor elderly are usually seen as being more needy, more deserving, and more grateful than poor children. Moreover, though blacks and whites do not differ in the way they rank the poor elderly and poor children, whites prefer the elderly by a larger amount than blacks, who rate the groups closer together.

In Chapter 3 we saw that the disabled elderly generally receive more support than disabled children. When we compare these groups in regression analyses (Table 5.2), the first point to be noted—here as in other age comparisons—is that age of the welfare group accounts for only about half as

Table 5.1: Variables That Account for 1 Percent or More of the
Variance in Support Differences Between Poor Elderly and
Poor Children[a, b]

Criterion Variable	Predictor Variables Accounting for 1 Percent or More of the Variance	Total R^2
Increase in services scale	Deservingness (1%); Need (2%); Race–(1%); Occupational prestige–(1%)	10%
Nutrition scale	Gratefulness (1%); Locus of responsibility (1%)	6%
Monetary distribution: nutrition	Need (1%); Deservingness (2%); Gratefulness (2%); Just world–(1%)	10%
Monetary distribution: education	Gratefulness (2%); Government aid (1%); Race (1%); Education–(3%); Age+(1%)	12%
Monetary distribution: transportation	Deservingness (3%); Gratefulness (3%); Race (3%)	12%
Monetary distribution: G M income	Need (1%); Deservingness (4%); Gratefulness (2%)	9%
Standardized index	Need (1%); Deservingness (5%); Gratefulness (5%); Race–(2%)	18%

a. Only those variables that contribute 1 percent or more to the total variance explained are listed. Thus, since the variables that contribute less than 1 percent are not listed, the percentages in parentheses do not add up to make the total R^2.
b. The plus or minus behind the demographic variables indicate the direction of the differences. For example, "age–" indicates that elderly people differentiate more between the two welfare groups than do younger people. "Education–" indicates that people with less education differentiate more than people with more education. Since whites were coded as "1" and blacks as "2," "race–" means that whites make larger differentiations than blacks.

much of the variance in support differences among the disabled as the poor. This probably results because the mean support for all disabled groups is so high that there is less variance to account for. A second point worth noting is that the predictor variables are not as consistently related to differences in support among the disabled as among the poor. However, differences in perceived deservingness and gratefulness account for at least 1 percent of the variance in differences in support for income and education services, while gratefulness accounts for this much variance for transportation and nutrition services. Differences in perceived need between the disabled elderly and disabled adults under 65 are related to differences in support for nutrition and general services. Unlike with poor elderly persons and poor children, race is not a reliable predictor of variance in support differences between disabled elderly persons and disabled children.

Let us turn now to the differences involving senior citizens and adults under 65. Chapter 3 showed that poor persons over 65 are supported more than poor persons under 65 for all services except education. As Table 5.3 illustrates, the elderly poor are consistently seen as more deserving than the poor under 65 and are sometimes seen as more needy. However, unlike with children, they are not seen as more grateful. Once again, whites make more of a differentiation in favor of

Table 5.2: Variables That Account for 1 Percent or More of the Variance in Support Differences Between Disabled Elderly and Disabled Children

Criterion Variable	Predictor Variables Accounting for 1 Percent or More of the Variance	Total R^2
Increase in services scale	Need (1%); Pleasant (3%)	9%
Nutrition scale	Gratefulness (1%); Race–(3%); Sex (1%); Education+(2%); Income+(1%)	12%
Monetary distribution: nutrition	Need (3%); Gratefulness (2%); Race (5%); Education+(2%); Occupational prestige (1%)	16%
Monetary distribution: education	Deservingness (1%); Gratefulness (2%); Know group member (1%)	7%
Monetary distribution: transportation	Pleasantness (1%); Gratefulness (1%); Age (1%)	5%
Monetary distribution: G M income	Deservingness (1%); Gratefulness (1%)	6%
Standardized index	Gratefulness (3%); Deservingness (1%); Need (1%)	9%

Table 5.3: Variables That Account for 1 Percent or More of the
            Variance in Support Differences Between Elderly Poor
            and Poor Adults Under 65

Criterion Variable	Predictor Variables Accounting for 1 Percent or More of the Variance	Total R^2
Increase in services scale	Need (1%); Deservingness (3%); Locus of Responsibility (1%); Income+(1%)	10%
Nutrition scale	Deservingness (3%); Locus of responsibility (1%); Government aid–(1%); Race–(4%); Income+(1%)	15%
Monetary distribution: nutrition	Deservingness (3%); Locus of responsibility (1%); Race–(1%); Income+(1%)	12%
Monetary distribution: education	Age+(2%)	5%
Monetary distribution: transportation	Deservingness (4%)	8%
Monetary distribution: G M income	Need (2%); Deservingness (5%); Pleasant (1%); Education–(1%)	14%
Standardized index	Deservingness (9%); Need (1%); Locus of responsibility (1%); Race–(2%); Income+(1%)	20%

the elderly than blacks do. Two new variables enter the
explanatory set when we consider the poor elderly and poor
adults under 65. The first is locus of responsibility. The
poor elderly are consistently seen as less responsible for their
fate than are younger adults. The second is income, and
here—independently of race—high-income groups make more
of a differentiation in favor of the elderly than do respondents with lower incomes.

The regression analyses comparing the disabled elderly and
disabled adults under 65 resulted in no consistent findings.
This may be because the two groups in question were rated
very close to each other on the support measures, as reported
in Chapter 3.

Let us now turn to comparison of adults under 65 and
children. Chapter 3 showed that, among the poor, children

are preferred to adults as targets of support for all services except education. Few predictors emerge consistently in the regression analysis. At most, differences in support are related to differences in perceived gratefulness for nutrition and transportation services; and in perceived need and deservingness for both income and nutrition services. The preference to support children over adults for nutrition and education programs is more marked among whites and persons of higher income than among blacks and persons of lower income. No consistent differences emerge in comparing disabled children and adults under 65.

We can summarize these findings quite simply:

(1) The elderly are preferred for support over children, and this may be because of differences in perceived gratefulness, deservingness, and need.

(2) The poor elderly are preferred for support over poor adults under 65, and this may be because they are seen as more

Table 5.4: Variables That Account for 1 Percent or More of the Variance in Support Differences Between Poor Children and Poor Adults Under 65

Criterion Variable	Predictor Variables Accounting for 1 Percent or More of the Variance	Total R^2
Increase in services scale	No variables accounted for 1% or more of the variance	3%
Nutrition scale	Gratefulness (1%); Race–(6%); Income+(1%)	13%
Monetary distribution: nutrition	Need (1%); Deservingness (1%); Gratefulness (1%); Race–(1%); Income+(1%)	10%
Monetary distribution: education	Race–(2%); Occupational prestige–(1%)	6%
Monetary distribution: transportation	Gratefulness (1%); Race+(1%)	6%
Monetary distribution: G M income	Need (2%); Deservingness (1%); Education–(1%); Income+(1%)	9%
Standardized index	Deservingness (1%); Income+(2%)	8%

deserving, more needy, and less responsible for their fate.

(3) Blacks and lower-income persons are in favor of more support than whites and higher-income persons, and they make smaller differentiations in the amount of support that they want to see given to welfare groups.

Explaining Differences Between the Poor and the Disabled

In Chapter 3 we saw that the disabled are frequently preferred for support over the poor. When the elderly disabled are contrasted with the elderly poor, as in Table 5.5, it can be seen that support preferences in favor of the elderly disabled are consistently related to differences in perceived need and are sometimes related to differences in perceived gratefulness and perhaps deservingness. No other variables are predictors with more than one support measure.

Table 5.5: Variables That Account for 1 Percent or More of the Variance in Support Differences Between Disabled Elderly and Elderly Poor

Criterion Variable	Predictor Variables Accounting for 1 Percent or More of the Variance	Total R^2
Increase in services scale	Need (1%)	5%
Nutrition scale	Need (1%); Likelihood (2%);	5%
Monetary distribution: nutrition	Need (2%); Gratefulness (2%); Occupational prestige (2%)	10%
Monetary distribution: education	Need (1%); Deservingness (2%); Gratefulness (5%); Government aid (1%)	12%
Monetary distribution: transportation	None	2%
Monetary distribution: G M income	Pleasant (1%); Race+(1%)	9%
Standardized index	Need (2%); Deservingness (1%); Gratefulness (2%)	9%

The disabled under 65 are usually supported more than poor persons under 65. Table 5.6 shows that differences in support are consistently related to differences in perceived deservingness. Half of the support measures are related to differences in locus of responsibility, with poor adults being seen as more responsible and being less supported. A new variable is also statistically significant with three of the support measures: Persons who think it is more likely they may become disabled are in favor of supporting the disabled more than the poor. As far as the demographic predictors are concerned, whites and high-income groups make more of a differentiation between the poor and the disabled than do blacks.

Table 5.6: Variables That Account for 1 Percent or More of the Variance in Support Differences Between Disabled Adults Under 65 and Poor Adults Under 65

Criterion Variable	Predictor Variables Accounting for 1 Percent or More of the Variance	Total R^2
Increase in services scale	Deservingness (1%); Pleasant (1%); Income+(1%)	7%
Nutrition scale	Deservingness (1%); Locus of responsibility (1%); Likelihood (3%); Race–(4%); Income+(2%); Occupational prestige+(2%)	19%
Monetary distribution: nutrition	Likelihood (2%); Deservingness (1%); Occupational prestige+(1%)	9%
Monetary distribution: education	Know group member (2%)	5%
Monetary distribution: transportation	Deservingness (1%); Locus of responsibility (1%); Race–(2%)	7%
Monetary distribution: G M income	Deservingness (3%); Occupational prestige+(1%)	9%
Standardized index	Deservingness (3%); Pleasant (2%); Locus of responsibility (1%); Likelihood (1%); Know (1%); Race–(2%); Income+(1%); Occupational prestige+(1%)	18%

When disabled and poor children are compared, Table 5.7 shows that disabled children are seen as more deserving and grateful and that this is related to a preference for supporting children who are disabled over children who are poor. Interestingly enough, disabled children are seen as less responsible for their plight than poor children, and this difference is also associated with greater support for disabled children. Race is again consistently related to differences in support, with whites making larger discriminations than blacks between disabled and poor children.

To summarize:

(1) The fact that disabled elderly persons are preferred over elderly poor may be related to their being seen as more needy.

(2) The fact that disabled adults under 65 and disabled children

Table 5.7: Variables That Account for 1 Percent of More of the Variance in Support Differences Between Disabled Children and Poor Children

Criterion Variable	Predictor Variables Accounting for 1 Percent or More of the Variance	Total R^2
Increase services scale	Deservingness (2%)	6%
Nutrition scale	Deservingness (1%); Gratefulness (2%); Race–(3%)	12%
Monetary distribution: nutrition	Race–(2%); Income–(3%)	9%
Monetary distribution: education	Deservingness (2%); Locus of responsibility	13%
Monetary distribution: transportation	Deservingness (1%); Gratefulness (1%); Locus of responsibility (1%); Race–(4%)	11%
Monetary distribution: G M income	Deservingness (4%); Pleasant (1%); Gratefulness (2%); Know (1%); Locus of responsibility (1%);	11%
Standardized index	Deservingness (5%); Gratefulness (1%); Locus of responsibility (3%); Race–(1%); Education (1%)	15%

receive more support than their poor counterparts may be related to their being seen as more deserving and less responsible for their plight.

Explaining Differences Between Disaster Victims and Poor or Disabled Adults

Chapter 3 showed that disaster victims are supported less than disabled persons for all services and less than poor persons for most services.

Table 5.8 compares the results from the difference score analysis between disaster victims and disabled persons. Differences in four psychological variables are related to differences in support: one is that disabled persons are seen as more deserving and more worthy of support; another is that respondents see themselves as more likely to be disabled than

Table 5.8: Variables That Account for 1 Percent or More of the Variance in Support Differences Between Disabled People and Disaster Victims

Criterion Variable	Predictor Variables Accounting for 1 Percent or More of the Variance	Total R^2
Increase in services scale	Likelihood (1%)	6%
Nutrition scale	None at 1% or over	4%
Monetary distribution: nutrition	Deserving (1%); Race (1%)	6%
Monetary distribution: education	Likelihood (4%); Just world-(1%)	11%
Monetary distribution: transportation	Deserving (2%); Pleasant (1%); Likelihood (3%); Just world-(1%); Income (2%)	13%
Monetary distribution: G M income	Deserving (3%); Income+(1%); Age+(1%)	8%
Standardized index	Deserving (4%); Pleasant (1%); Likelihood (2%); Just world-(1%)	15%

to be victims of a disaster; a third is that the disabled are seen as more pleasant. The final psychological variable helps explain why some persons support disaster victims over the disabled. Those who believe the world to be just are more likely to support disaster victims over the disabled.

Table 5.9 compares the results from the difference score analysis between poor people and disaster victims. The differences in support are related to the same four variables to which differences in support for disabled people and disaster victims are related. One new variable emerges: The fact that more respondents know poor people than know disaster victims is related to support differences between the groups.

Table 5.9: Variables That Account for 1 Percent or More of the Variance in Support Differences Between Poor People and Disaster Victims

Criterion Variable	Predictor Variables Accounting for 1 Percent or More of the Variance	Total R^2
Increase in services scale	Deservingness (1%); Pleasant (1%); Likelihood (1%); Know (1%)	6%
Nutrition scale	Deservingness (4%); Likelihood (2%); Know (3%); Race+(1%); Pleasant (1%)	11%
Monetary distribution: nutrition	Deservingness (6%); Gratefulness (1%); Income (1%); Likelihood (1%); Occupational prestige (2%); Education (1%); Age-(1%)	14%
Monetary distribution: education	Deservingness (4%); Likelihood (1%); Education (3%); Income (1%); Age-(1%); Just world-(1%)	13%
Monetary distribution: transportation	Deservingness (4%); Pleasant (2%); Gratefulness (2%); Likelihood (1%); Know (1%); Just world-(1%); Education+(2%); Income+(1%)	15%
Monetary distribution: G M Income	Deservingness (4%); Pleasant (2%); Know (1%); Just world-(1%); Income (2%); Age-(	12%
Standardized index	Deservingness (8%); Pleasant (2%); Likelihood (2%); Know (2%); Just world-(1%)	23%

To summarize: Differences in support between disaster victims and the poor or disabled are most strongly associated with differences in perceived deservingness, and are also associated with differences in attributed pleasantness and the likelihood that respondents will suffer from the same plight as the welfare group members. For the first time in comparisons between groups, belief in a just world is associated with support. Those who believe the world to be a just place are more likely to support disaster victims.

An Overview of Results from the Difference Score Analyses

The variable most strongly related to differences in support is differences in attributed deservingness. The issue with deservingness is whether it should be considered a variable that explains support or a variable that is merely a synonym for support. This is an issue to which we shall return in Chapter 6.

Support for the elderly is also regularly associated with the perception that they are more needy than other age groups, and the preference for supporting the elderly disabled over the poor elderly is related to the former being seen as more needy than the latter. Although attributed need may play a special role in mediating support for the elderly, its role for other groups may be different.

The low support for adults under 65 is probably related, not only to the low level of deservingness attributed to them, but also to the cognition that they are responsible for their fate. This same variable may also explain the preference to support disabled children over poor children.

The likelihood that one may come to share the fate of a particular welfare group is not often related to support, except with disaster victims who are supported least of all and whom respondents do not think they will emulate. Another variable related to disaster victims but to no other group is the psychological belief in a just world. Persons who believe the world to be a just place seem to prefer disaster victims more than persons who believe it to be unjust. The possibility exists, therefore, that the low support given to disaster victims is associated with a different set of predictors than is the support given to other groups.

THE EXPERIMENT

Experiments are conducted to answer the causal question: If X is deliberately made to vary, will Y vary with it? In the case of our experiment, the Xs are whether someone described in a vignette has one of four levels of poverty (none, marginal, severe-acute [i.e., short term], severe-chronic [i.e., long term]); one of four levels of disability (none, marginal, severe-acute, severe-chronic); is a relatively young or old adult (under 35 vs. over 65); and is or is not responsible for the events that led him to become poor or disabled. Details of how the vignette characters were developed and operationalized were given in Chapter 2. The major purpose of the experiment was to test how the above characteristics of hypothetical individuals affect the level of support respondents are willing to give. The index of support was described in Chapter 2, and it is worth reiterating that the measure is most heavily weighted by two items: the respondents' willingness to pay more taxes and to attend a public meeting.

Some of the manipulated characteristics in the experiment overlap with characteristics that earlier analyses in this chapter suggested may be causal. In particular, the locus of causality variable may have been important in mediating support decisions for adults and children, particularly if they are poor, and it is explored in the experiment. The need factor also emerged as potentially significant in earlier explanatory analyses and is explored in the experiment in the difference between marginal and severe levels of chronic and acute disability and poverty. However, some of the variables studied earlier could not be included in the experiment, particularly attributed pleasantness, gratitude, or the likelihood one would become a member of a particular welfare group. Moreover, the distinction between acute and chronic poverty and disability was not included in the survey part of the study but was included in the experiment. It is an important variable in that it permits us to assess the degree to which a factor in helping is the "victim's" ability to become self-sustaining.

Thus, the experiment does not have perfect overlap with the survey in the explanatory variables studied, and could not have because, practically speaking, (1) experiments are restricted in the number of independent variables that can be manipulated; and (2) the explanatory variables were not selected for experimental study on the basis of the results from the correlational analyses in the other section of the survey. The experiment and survey were conducted simultaneously.

Main Effect Results for Vignette Characteristics

The analysis of variance shows a main effect of poverty that accounts for about 1 percent of the variance in the support index. The means are: no poverty, 46.59; marginal poverty, 52.30; acute poverty, 53.08; and chronic poverty, 53.76. Thus, respondents discriminate in their support between living without poverty and living with any kind of poverty. (It might be thought that the lack of discrimination among types of poverty is due to a failure of the manipulation. Evidence will be presented later that throws doubt on such an interpretation and instead suggests that the increasing severity of one's poverty is not important, in general, in eliciting more support.)

The variance analysis also results in a main effect of disability that accounts for about 8 percent of the variance. The means are: no disability, 38.16; marginal disability, 51.21; acute disability 55.18; and chronic disability, 61.24. Thus, the Chicago public clearly discriminates between types of disability, and the severity and expected duration of a disability each elicit greater reported willingness to act on behalf of the disabled person. Moreover, it is worth noting that differences in the severity and permanence of a disability seem to elicit greater support differences than is the case with poverty. Disability is probably a more salient and powerful cue for causing support than is poverty.

The level of support also depends on the age of the vignette characters, with older persons receiving greater support than younger persons. The respective means are 54.22 and 48.45, and this difference accounts for about 1 percent of the variance in the support index used in the experiment.

Locus of responsibility is almost as strong a cause of support as disability, accounting for about 7 percent of the explainable variance. Persons who caused their own plights receive considerably less support than those who are not responsible for their plights (mean support scores = 42.58 and 60.28 respectively).

Interaction Effects Among Vignette Characteristics

Interpretation of the above main effects needs qualification because every independent variable enters into at least one interaction with another independent variable. The most powerful interaction, accounting for about 3 percent of the variance, is between poverty and disability. However, this interaction—like the interaction of poverty and causality which accounts for 1 percent of the variance—is best interpreted in terms of the three-way interaction involving poverty, disability, and locus of responsibility, an interaction that also accounts for about 1 percent of the variance.

The means for the three-way interaction are plotted in Figure 5.2 for vignette characters who caused their own plight, and in Figure 5.3 for characters whose plight was externally caused. If we look first at Figure 5.2, we find that when the poverty and disability are self-caused, support increases monotonically with the degree of disability for all low-poverty groups. However, the rate of increase in support is greatest for the nonpoor, followed by the acutely poor, the marginally poor, and finally the chronically poor. In other words, self-caused disability is likely to bring more public support if individuals do not also have self-caused poverty. To illustrate, chronically disabled vignette characters who are not poor receive a mean support level of 65.49, whereas chronically disabled vignette characters who are also chronically poor receive a mean support level of only 44.35.

Before one draws any conclusions about the "heartless public" that does not want to support multiproblem adults who have caused their own chronic disability and poverty, we have to note another feature of Figure 5.2. Among those who are not disabled (the left side of the figure), poor individuals receive more support than relatively more affluent persons. The discrimination seems to be against multiproblem individuals who have caused their own multiple plights rather than against persons who have caused just their own poverty.

Figure 5.3 shows that, among persons who are *not* responsible for their plight, it is no longer the case that the disabled poor receive less support than the disabled who are more affluent. Instead, once the plight is other-caused, support is consistently high, and there is little differentiation in the mean level of support regardless of either (1) the level of poverty or disability, or (2) the combined conditions of poverty and disability.

The only other interaction involving vignette characteristics that accounts for 1 percent of the variance is the interaction of poverty and age. This has already been discussed in Chapter 3, for the same effect was obtained in the

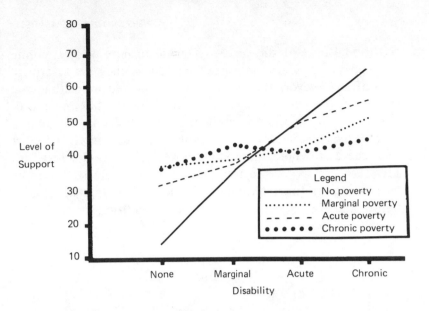

Fig. 5.2: The poverty by disability interaction within the
          self caused condition

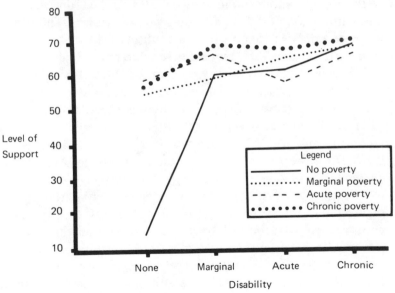

Fig. 5.3: The poverty by disability interaction within the
          other caused condition

traditional part of the survey. To recapitulate briefly, young and old persons are supported equally if they are relatively well-off. However, the elderly are supported more than the young if they are in any state of poverty, but most pronouncedly when the poverty is marginal. Indeed, for younger characters, marginal poverty evokes no increase in support over the case where there is no poverty. But both short- and long-term poverty result in substantially increased support for young victims, although the level of support remains below that for older victims in similar conditions.

SUMMARY

The descriptive section of the survey permits us to learn the welfare group and respondent attributes associated with differences in the support for particular welfare groups. The experiment permits us to learn whether a subset of these variables can cause differences in the support offered to individuals.

We learn from the survey that the disabled adults, in general, are seen as more deserving, needy, and grateful than their poor age counterparts; that they are seen as less responsible for their fate; and that respondents believe that disability is more likely to happen to them than poverty. We learn from the experiment that increases in the severity and permanence of disability and plight caused by others can lead to greater support. We suggest, therefore, that the greater support for disabled adults when compared to their poor counterparts may be due to five attributes that the disabled are seen to have, all of which may increase support. They are seen as more needy, grateful, and deserving by persons who do not believe them responsible for their fate and who think that the fate of the disabled is more likely to befall them than the fate of becoming poor. However, it is clear that support is not offered to the disabled in an undiscerning manner. Elderly disabled persons, for instance, are less supported for educational services than disabled persons under 65. Our speculation is that respondents want to meet needs that will enhance the independence of the disabled, whether the needs are for mobility (as with transportation services), financial aid (income guarantee programs), or food (nutrition services). They will be less ready to support programs that do not reach this goal; e.g., education might not achieve the goal of independence for the disabled elderly but might do so for younger disabled persons.

The data suggest that the variables explaining the support for disabled children or poor children are somewhat different from the corresponding variables with older persons. Though disabled children are seen as more deserving, grateful, and less responsible for their fate than poor children (sic!), this is only associated with greater support for transportation, income guarantee, and education services. With both nutrition measures, poor children are preferred over disabled, especially when the single item measuring the willingness to pay more taxes is examined. Our speculation is that disabled children will only be preferred over poor children for services to the extent that respondents believe the children have alternatives. Realizing that disability costs money, respondents want to protect the income of parents, and make sure the child has a chance, via education and transportation to be as independent as possible. But they balk at the idea of the government taking over all responsibilities, including less costly ones like feeding, which parents ought to be able to provide, assuming they are not close to being destitute. Where families are close to being destitute, respondents are willing to support basic bodily needs, which is why poor children are preferred over disabled children for nutritional services.

The poor elderly are seen as being more in need and less likely to have caused their own fate, than poor adults under 65. The experiment indicates that respondents may not use the severity and permanence of poverty as a potent cue in assigning support. Certainly, severity and permanence are less powerful cues than when they relate to disability and not poverty. However, locus of causality is a very powerful cue, and our speculation is that this is the major cause of the greater support offered to the poor elderly over the poor under 65. But—as with age differences among the disabled— need may play a role. Two points about the help offered to the poor elderly deserve comment. First, the public is more willing to finance basic life-supporting systems for the elderly poor—like nutrition and income guarantees—than less needed services like education. Second, the absence of a significant interaction between the age of someone in need and whether his or her plight is or is not self-caused suggests that elderly persons whose poverty is not of their own making are not helped to a noticeably greater degree because they are victims and are also old. They are helped more because they have each attribute; but the variables appear to combine additively rather than in some more complex fashion.

Poor adults under 65 are seen by most respondents in the survey as being responsible for their plight, and in the experiment such perceptions of responsibility are linked to support. Only where the opportunity exists to escape this plight, as with educational services, are poor adults supported to any degree. However, the experimental results suggest that if the poverty of adults of working age is seen to be externally caused, then public support would increase and no special stigma would be attached by others to being poor *and* of working age. In the latter respect, it is worth noting from the experiment that self-caused poverty among young persons is still associated with more support than is offered to the nonpoor. Some help is offered them. It is obvious that the general public's attribution of the cause of poverty is not universally shared. Since respondents who are black or with low income are more likely to advocate services for poor adults, it is possible that self-interest plays a role in some persons' advocacy of help for poor adults. However, it may not play a major role, for blacks and low-income respondents assigned the same rank ordering as others to support for the seven welfare groups across a variety of services. The evidence in favor of self-interest is minimal, based on differences in means across racial groups even though these means had the same rank ordering.

Disaster victims received least help of all in the survey, and in this chapter we show that respondents believe that disasters are not likely to happen to them. Moreover, the persons most likely to support disaster victims are people who believe that the world is a just place, a belief that is usually associated with low levels of absolute support. One wonders whether disaster victims would receive so little support if our respondents had lived on the San Andreas Fault or in a hurricane zone. One also wonders if they would receive so little support if their primary supporters were not also the people who believe that most suffers get what is just anyway.

NOTE

1. The multiple regression analyses were run with just the social, just the psychological, and just the welfare group attribute data to test whether the relationship of predictor variables to the support criteria varied dramatically as a function of the set of predictors. In no case did this occur. Hence, the results presented here are for analyses of the total set of predictors.

Chapter 6

THE IMPLICATIONS OF A HOMOGENEOUS

AND DISCERNING PUBLIC

The task of this book was to describe the differences in public support for seven social welfare groups and the extent to which various segments of the public differed in their support. A further aim was to explain any differences in support that might emerge. This chapter summarizes the major findings and discusses their implications.

WHO SHOULD BE HELPED?

Public preferences appear, in general, to be more favorable toward supporting some groups than others. Overall, the disabled receive more support than the poor, and support seems to be greater the more serious the poverty and disability. Also, the elderly receive more support than do children and adults under 65. On the average, the disabled elderly are the most preferred group, and poor adults under 65 are least preferred. In addition, a chronic condition is often more likely to elicit support than an acute condition, particularly where disability is concerned. Disaster victims usually receive low support rankings.

A more interesting and important finding is that, although the public appears to have these general preferences, they are not applied undiscerningly from one service to the next. Rather, support for a group is made contingent on the particular nature of the service in question. In other words, support preferences may best be understood as linked to groups via particular services. While the condition of disability appears to be the criterion determining support for transportation programs, the criterion of age appears to be more important for determining support for nutrition programs, with most support being assigned to the elderly. Though poor adults of working age are not at all supported for most services, they are preferred to all others for job-related educational services. Though disabled children receive very low support for nutrition services, they receive very high support for transportation services and for a general increase in services. The elderly receive low ratings of support for education programs but high ratings for nutrition and income services. These are not stereotypical preferences applied indiscriminately from one program to the next but rather preferences made contingent on the service being requested for a particular group.

Three implications of these findings can be examined. They have implications for the interpretation of the survey research question on support for "social welfare"; for the argument that the public is an indiscriminant source to consult as one input in the policy formulation process; and for the claims that have been made about which groups are supported.

Implications for Support for "Social Welfare"

It is a common practice in survey research to ask a question about whether the respondents think the United States spends too much, not enough, or just the right amount for "social welfare." Our findings have implications for understanding the inadequacies of this procedure which has probably contributed to creating the widespread impression that the public is not willing to support people in need. The question can give misleading results because the respondents' referent is not clear. Does welfare mean poor adults under 65—one of the least often helped groups in the present study—or does it mean the disabled elderly—one of the most often helped groups in this study? If respondents had the poor under 65 in mind when they answered the global welfare question of past research, this would give a pessimistic underestimate of public willingness to help the disabled elderly. Similarly, an overly optimistic view of willingness to help poor adults would result if respondents had the disabled elderly in mind. The point is we do not know which group they had in mind so that responses to the global question of past researchers are inherently ambiguous.

In addition to not specifying particular welfare groups, the global question does not specify programs, that is, respondents are asked whether more or less money should be spent on *welfare* without particular welfare *services* being mentioned. The present study suggests that support for particular welfare groups depends on the service for which support is asked. We think, therefore, that responses to the global welfare question would change if it were worded in terms of specific programs. The presumption in the typical survey question about welfare is that the welfare groups and services are clear to respondents or that the similarity between welfare groups and services exceeds the differences between them. The clarity issue remains to be demonstrated, and our study indicates that the assumption of similarity is hardly tenable. Thus, the typical contextless question about welfare support may be more misleading than useful.

Implications for Bases of Discernment

The findings have implications for those who would argue that the public should not be consulted in the policy formulation process because public comprehension of social welfare groups and their needs is simplistic and undifferentiated, making public preferences irrelevant as one input in policy determination. The data reviewed here show that the public *does* differentiate among groups and that this differentiation does not appear to be based on global images of groups. Rather, it appears to be based on reflections about the special needs of different groups and the services that might meet these needs. One can, of course, still argue that public opinion should not be consulted and used as one input in policy-making, but the reason cannot be used that the public has global, indiscriminant preferences.

It is still not clear whether the public makes these discernments in every-day life or only in situations where judgments are requested. It is also not clear on what basis discernments are made. This is in part due to the fact that we had not anticipated such differences and had planned to use the services as replicates rather than as "dependent variables" in their own right. Thus, our discussion of why the Chicago public makes the program discriminations it does must necessarily be tentative.

One possibility is that discernments are made on the basis of whether a program permits *meeting essential needs*. For instance, transportation is probably more crucial a service for the disabled than for the poor, and the preferential treatment that the disabled get is more pronounced for transportation services than for any others. Similarly, it can be argued that the elderly tend to be more dependent on nonfamily members for basic life-supporting programs like food and income. These were also programs for which they received most support. Also, it can be argued that adults under 65 will particularly benefit from more education which might bring them and their families to financial independence. This was, in fact, how the data turned out.

A second possibility is that the public discriminates among groups and programs hoping *to maximize individual independence* whenever possible. Thus, we find a stronger preference for education services for working age adults over other age groups and for children over the elderly. Thus, also, we find a stronger preference for the disabled to receive transportation services, which will, it can be argued, result in greater independence for them. There may be in this an element of cost consciousness, but there may also be a simple desire to see as many persons as possible achieve the maximum possible freedom.

The third possibility is that the Chicago public may make its support decisions contingent on whether a particular group *has alternative sources of help* for the service provided by a particular program. While we cannot yet determine which of these possibilities is correct, we can draw one important conclusion. This is that the general public does not have a general attitude about support which colors all of its decisions. Instead, there may well be different reasons for preferring to support particular services for some groups over other groups. We advance the above three possibilities as hypotheses and suggest that research is needed to test these hypotheses to understand more about the conditions under which discernments are manifested.

Implications for Claims

Chapter 1 presented frequently heard claims by commentators that some groups are either especially preferred or not preferred. Our findings show some of these claims to be either too simplistic or wrong. For example, Butler (1975) claims that the elderly are not well supported: "Society seems to be saying, 'They're old—they don't need much in the way of services. Don't waste resources on them. Or give them a little service now and then. That will keep them quiet and we'll have done enough' " (1975: 140).

The present data clearly indicate that the impression of Butler is not shared by the general public, for willingness to support the elderly was very high for most services. In the vignettes, when two people were described who were similar except for age, the greater support almost invariably went to the elderly person rather than to the person under 65. But support for the elderly was not unlimited. For education services, it was noteworthy that the elderly were ranked last in support when compared to other groups. The answer to why the public is less willing to help the elderly with education services might suggest the conditions under which Butler might be right. One speculation is the following: Nutrition, income, and transportation are probably seen by most Americans as basic life maintainers. Education, on the other hand, is probably not seen as a basic life-supporting system, especially for the elderly. It may be that high support for the elderly is restricted to what is inferred to be life-supporting systems. Perhaps the services to which commentators such as Butler implicitly refer when they speak of the low support for the elderly are services that the public sees as more like education than nutrition.

Butler's referent for the global "elderly" category is not known. He may be right about low support if his referent is certain groups of elderly persons—for example, middle- or upper-class elderly. We do not know. We looked only at support for the poor and disabled elderly, and for these groups support is generally high—but not indiscriminant.

Our data also challenge Carter et al.'s claim (1973) that children are especially preferred and are supported more than other age groups. Among the disabled, both adults over 65 and under 65 receive more support than children on the overall summary scale of support. And among the poor, the elderly usually receive more support than children. The dependence of support on programs being considered suggests that Carter might be correct for some interventions (e.g., foster care), and, in fact, in the present study, children do receive significantly more support than the elderly for education services. And for transportation services and a general increase in services, disabled children receive about the same amount of support as do the disabled elderly. However, both groups of children receive significantly more support only for education services.

On the basis of informal sampling, it is our impression that many persons other than Carter believe that children are especially supported. It is certainly a favorite technique of experienced charity seekers to present pictures and verbal descriptions of charming children who suffer from some plight. Thus, we are presented at Christmas with children who will not receive presents. We see the Easter seal child and the muscular distrophy child. Rarely, if ever, do we have the elderly person who gets no Christmas presents, the Easter seal senior citizen, the arteriosclerotic grandfather. The strategies of charity seekers may well have contributed to the common belief that children are especially supported. However, no social science evidence of which we are aware exists to support the belief. Our own evidence contradicts it.

Though overall, children are least preferred among the disabled age groups and preferred less than the elderly among the poor, this does not mean that they are seen as any less pleasant and deserving or any more responsible for their plight. In fact, our analyses show they are not. However, they are seen to be less needy than older persons. Our guess is that children receive less support than elderly groups, not because of traits ascribed to them, but because they are perceived to have easily available alternative sources of aid—parents or other caretakers who should take responsibility for them. On the other hand, disabled adults and poor adults over 65 have fewer alternative sources of aid. If these speculations are true, we might expect to find very high levels of support when a child, e.g., an orphan, has no alternative sources of support. A task of future research is to learn whether the support given to children may depend most of all on the alternative sources of support that are easily available to children.

Claims have also been made that the American public is particularly supportive of the disabled (Berkowitz, 1976). In general, these claims appear to be correct, but they are somewhat oversimplified because we have seen that disability is not always the major criterion of support for every service. For nutrition services, for example, the age of the group seems to determine that the elderly—both disabled *and* poor—should receive the most support. Claiming that "the disabled" as a group are most likely to be supported may be too simplistic for another reason. Disabled children, the elderly, and adults under 65 are not always supported co-equally. The public seems to believe that different age groups among the disabled may have different needs for different services. Thus, for example, elderly persons who are disabled get a high rating for nutrition services, but children who are disabled get one of the lowest ratings for nutrition services.

Much support is also claimed for disaster victims (Maynes, 1974). Yet, for service after service, respondents gave disaster victims less support than most other groups except, sometimes, poor adults under 65. This finding will surprise many as it did us. It may be that if respondents had been asked about other services—for example, emergency housing or crisis counseling—support would have been higher. Our guess is that this might not have been the case, for one could argue that the services that *were* asked about are basic "life-maintaining" and "self-sufficiency-restoring" ones: "food assistance programs" after disaster strikes, "special transportation services right after disasters," and education service to help victims "learn how to repair the damages done" by the disaster.

The common consensus in most social welfare texts (e.g., Axinn and Levin, 1975; Bremner, 1956; Brieland et al., 1975) is that the public is least supportive of services for the poor of working age—in other words, poor adults under 65. Our findings show that, in general, this is the case, and respondents seem less willing to support services for this group than for others. However, it is not invariably true. They are the most preferred group for education services.

At the core of the findings on "who should be helped," there exists *no simple pattern* of most to least preferred social welfare group. Thus, any claim about one group being "*the* most preferred" has to be qualified in terms of the service for which it is supported.

Opinions Versus Behavior

A crucial issue is to decide whether reported willingness to support social services will translate into actions that reflect the reported priorities among the seven welfare groups. It is well known that the correlation between opinions and behaviors caries considerably. The two major conditions under which opinions are closely related to behaviors are when the opinions are (1) "behavioroid" and (2) specific in their referent (Fishbein and Ajzen, 1975; Kelman, 1974). For example, the first type of support measure in this study is clearly "behavioroid," being based on willingness to distribute money to the groups and actually involving the specific allocation of play money. In addition, respondents were not asked opinion questions about *global* groups (e.g., "the elderly"), as do many attitude surveys (Harris and Associates, 1975; Schiltz, 1970). Instead, they were asked questions about willingness to assign funds to more specific groups (e.g., the physically disabled elderly, disaster victims, physi-

cally disabled children). Respondents related their support to
specific services (e.g., Meals on Wheels, which was the nutrition service for the elderly).

Moreover, in the experimental section of the survey,
respondents answered questions on their willingness to have
their taxes raised, to attend meetings, and to write their
congressmen in support of specific welfare groups. The results from the experimental section closely corresponded
with the results from the traditional survey section. Such
correspondence suggests, but does not prove, that our measures of support have face validity and may be more closely
related to behavior than is often the case in survey research.

WHO HELPS WHOM?

Respondent groups differ in their level of support for
social welfare groups but not in their patterns of support for
these groups. With respect to the *level of support,* blacks
offer more support than whites, especially if they are males
over 50 and low income. Whites are less supportive in general,
though younger whites are more supportive than older
whites, and low-income whites are more supportive than
upper-income whites.

With respect to the *pattern of support* for the seven
welfare groups, the preference rankings hardly differ with
race, income, sex, or age groups. For service after service, the
striking similarity which appears indicates that the Chicago
public is homogeneous with respect to which groups it prefers to support for specific services. The differences in *level*
of support, which suggest some heterogeneity between
respondent groups, are trivial in magnitude when compared
to the consistent similarity in ranking between groups.

The demonstrated similarity is with respect to preferences
within the welfare domain. The data do not permit generali-

zation beyond this domain. Hence, we have nothing to say about whether the various segments of the public we examined would give similar rankings if, say, they were asked to rank the desirability of spending for social welfare as opposed to spending for defense, pollution control, or the like. The results also should not be generalized beyond the welfare groups and services that we studied. It is not at all clear, for example, whether relative preferences would stay the same for services that some respondent groups would see as luxuries. A common feature of our services, education perhaps excepted, is that they were all basic to meeting essential needs.

With these caveats in mind, we can conclude that the welfare domain seems to be one of those areas where it is justified to speak of "public opinion" as opposed to the "opinion of different publics." That is, in many domains of public policy, the difference between segments of the public are very striking and preclude speaking usefully about public opinion as though this were a common attribute. As far as preference for welfare groups is concerned, there really does seem to be one public opinion.

Implications of a Homogeneous Public

This conclusion has considerable implications both for policy-makers and for political theorists. A belief shared by many political scientists, policy-makers, and market researchers is that population subgroups hold diverse views on a wide variety of issues due to the groups' different backgrounds, life styles, and ideologies. Whether it be the concept of "segmentation" for marketing researchers or "interest group politics" for political scientists, the stress is on different publics within the general American public and sources of division which drive them apart. Surely, in many areas of American life, these concepts apply, and the various constituencies within the public are at cross-purposes—for example, in the area of pollution control, we have those in favor of the environmentalists pitted against those in favor of the industrialists; in the consumer arena, we have, for example, avid smokers who support the tobacco farmers and cigarette manufacturers against the usually nonsmoking proponents of the American Cancer Society's philosophy. Such divisions are an expected and accepted part of American life. Thus, it would not have been hard to imagine that similar divisions would be found in patterns of support for services for social groups.

No such divisions among support patterns of different constituencies within the public are found. Instead, in the social welfare domain, the Chicago public is found to be homogeneous. What makes the homogeneity all the more impressive is the following: As we pointed out in an earlier section, respondents' rank ordering of preferences among welfare groups differ from service to service. That finding is based on an examination of the preferences across *all* respondents. However, when we examine the preferences of constituencies within the respondents, we find that male and female, black and white, young and old, rich and poor, all have similar patterns of support, *patterns that differ in the same way for each service.* Such consistency in differing patterns of support across seven different support measures for seven social welfare groups bears testimony to a rather remarkable degree of homogeneity. Not only is the Chicago public discerning but it is homogeneously discerning.

The conclusion regarding the level of homogeneity among the public holds important implications for policy-makers and program planners, for it is easier to implement tax-related policies where a strong concensus exists among Americans than where there are significant divisions. For example, policy-makers who favor education programs for poor adults under 65 might reasonably expect to see their support reciprocated by the public en masse. They might expect to find rather consistent resistance to several other services. By knowing in advance about the resistance to expect and possible reasons for it, they may better plan a strategy to gain support. Having a clearer understanding about the conditions under which there may be public resistance or support could be especially useful for policy development and program planning.

The findings on the homogeneous public have implications for those who would argue that the public should not be consulted in the social welfare policy-making process. One argument is based on the fact that there is not one public but rather many publics and that they are at such cross-purposes that any consultation would be of little use. As the data have shown, this does not seem to be the case. Indeed, the opposite is the case. Anyone who wants to use public opinion as one input for social service policy options can anticipate an undivided public. The activist advocates for the different groups may be divided, but the general public is not.

The degree of homogeneity among the public comes as a surprise. It is not at all clear how different subgroups within the public come to have such homogeneous preference rankings. It suggests that the American public at large is subject during its socialization to the same cultural forces which indicate the groups that most deserve financial support. Certainly, the aid that is offered cannot be understood in terms of narrow immediate self-interests, for otherwise poor persons who are young would hardly support the disabled elderly over poor adults under 65. To be sure, it could be argued that they themselves may fear becoming old and disabled or that they fear having dependent relatives who are old and disabled. Yet this explanation does not seem to be true; otherwise, support would have been more systematically related to the likelihood of becoming a member of one of the welfare groups and of knowing someone in one of the welfare groups. While it is in some ways not very intellectually satisfying to invoke an explanatory construct like "being members of a common socialization environment," the consistency in preference rankings across respondent groups makes any other explanation difficult. Whether this consistency would still be manifested if real dollars were being distributed to real people remains an intriguing but unanswered question that goes beyond the scope of this project.

WHY DOES THE PUBLIC HELP WHOM IT HELPS?

Both the experimental and the descriptive sections of the survey attempted to explain differences in support for the seven groups. The descriptive section did this through analyses which showed how differences in support for groups are associated with differences in attributes of respondents and welfare groups: (1) the respondents' level of belief in a just world, (2) their perception of the likelihood of a social welfare group's plight happening to them, (3) whether they know a member of a particular welfare group, (4) whether they have received government aid, (5) how they perceive the welfare group's need, (6) the group's deservingness, (7) pleasantness, (8) gratefulness, and (9) whether or not they perceive the group to be responsible for its plight.

The experimental section of the survey tested causes of support through a randomized experiment in which respondents were read vignettes describing people at different levels of need and condition. Specifically, the attributes of the vignette characters that were experimentally manipulated were: age (over or under 65), the nature of the condition (poor v. disabled), the severity of the condition (absent, present at marginal levels, present at high acute levels, present at high chronic levels), and the reason for an individual being in this condition (self-caused responsibility for plight v. other-caused).

The reason for using both a traditional survey and an experiment has been discussed in detail in Chapter 2. To briefly summarize, surveys are superior for *describing* people's opinions and examining associations between opinions, whereas experiments are more useful for *explaining* opinions since, among a host of other reasons, they make the temporal order of cause and effect clear. We wanted to combine the greater power of the randomized experiment for making causal inferences with the greater descriptive fidelity of the traditional survey. Summarizing the explanatory findings from both the survey and the experiment, we learned that:

(1) The greater support for disabled adults over poor adults for most services may be due to the fact that they are seen as more needy, grateful, and deserving and as less responsible for their condition. Moreover, respondents believe that they themselves are more likely to become disabled than poor.

(2) The greater support for disabled children over poor children for transportation, education, and income services may be related to the fact that they are seen as more deserving, grateful, and less responsible for their fate than poor children. For nutrition measures, poor children are preferred over disabled children, and our speculation is that respondents believe that disabled children have other alternatives for nutrition and resist the idea of social serrvices taking over an unnecessary responsibility. The other three services may have been seen as especially useful to give the disabled child the chance to become as independent as possible.

(3) The greater support for the elderly poor over poor adults under 65 may be due to the perception that the elderly have greater need and are not responsible for their condition. From the experiment, we learned that locus of causality of plight is a very powerful determinant of support, and we think that this is the major cause of greater support for the elderly poor over poor adults under 65.

(4) The overall lower support for poor adults under 65 is quite strongly linked to the fact that they are seen to be responsible for their plight. However, two points are noteworthy. First, when respondents feel they can help poor adults under 65 to escape their plight by providing them with education services, support is very high. Second, in the experiment, when the poverty of adults under 65 is clearly shown to be externally caused, support increases.

(5) The low support for disaster victims seems to be related to the fact that respondents do not know disaster victims nor think such a plight could happen to them. Moreover, the supporters of disaster victims are those who think the world is a just place and people get what they deserve. These "just worlders" give more support to disaster victims than to other groups, presumably because they think the condition of these victims is "unjust" and should be alleviated whereas the condition of the other groups is somehow more "just" and should not be alleviated.

The findings regarding reasons for support are more tentative than the other findings. This point needs elaboration. In the correlational analysis, we were able to show an association between differences in support and differences in the possible explanatory variables of gratefulness, locus of responsibility for plight, likelihood of becoming a welfare group member, and so on. However, association does not by itself imply causation. For example, from the traditional survey section of the study, we learn that the difference in support between elderly poor persons and poor adults under 65 is related to the fact that respondents perceive adults under 65 to be more responsible for their plight than elderly adults. However, on the strength of that correlational association alone, we would not be able to determine whether the presumed cause (i.e., locus of responsibility for plight) preceded the effect (i.e., support) or whether support came first followed by a justification for support.

It is at this point in our concern about cause that the experimental manipulation in the vignettes becomes important. In the vignettes we can be confident that the cause preceded the effect since varying the presumed cause and measuring the hoped-for effect were under our control. Moreover, we carefully tailored the description of the vignette characters so that they were described identically with one exception—each had a different locus of responsibility for plight, one being self-caused, the other externally caused. The fact that the vignette characters who caused their own plight received less support than those whose plight was caused externally strongly suggests that differences in the locus of responsibility can cause differences in support. However, the explanatory findings in this study are necessarily tentative for two major reasons. First, we were not able to test each potential explanatory variable in both the experimental and traditional sections of the survey as we tested locus of responsibility. Indeed, an important reason for conducting an experiment *after* an initial survey is that the survey can teach us which variables to include in an experimental test. However, for practical reasons we had to conduct the experiment simultaneously with the rest of the survey. Also, practically speaking, only a limited number of variables can be manipulated in an experiment. Second, even if we had been able to include all of the important potential explanatory variables in the experiment, there would still have been an inferential leap in concluding that the experimental results directly elucidate the explanatory processes that operated in the survey. The leap arises because the experiment tests forces that *can* cause differences in support; but it does not prove that these forces were in the respondents' minds when they responded to the survey. Nonetheless, a close correspondence of results across the survey and experiment strongly suggests that the correlations between variables in the survey may reflect any causal forces between the same variables that are shown to be operating in the experiment.

Evidence of Further Discernment

Just as members of the public are discerning about who should be supported for what services, the data show that they are also discerning about *why* different groups should be supported. Only one variable emerged again and again in the descriptive survey section as a correlate of differences in the support offered to welfare groups. This is a measure of the extent to which groups are seen to differ in deservingness. The very generality of the relationship between deservingness and support must make one suspect that deservingness and support may form a common factor instead of being two unique constructs (i.e., being deserving may mean being deserving of *support*). Thus, it may be that deservingness is more usefully conceptualized as an indirect measure of support rather than as an independent determinant of support.

Other than deservingness, the public does not seem to use any single attribute to decide why it will support one group over another. Instead, need and perhaps gratitude are important for supporting the elderly over others; a low likelihood of being in a disaster is important for supporting disaster victims less than others; and a belief that poor adults over 65 have caused their own plight is important for supporting these adults less than others.

More important than such individual attributes of the welfare group or of the person responding to the group may be the public's bases of judgments about *which groups* should receive *which services*. We made the case in an earlier section that judgment may rest on (1) whether a program permits *meeting essential needs,* (2) whether a program *maximizes individual independence,* and (3) whether a group has *alternative sources of help.*

For example, disabled children may have alternative sources of help for nutrition services, but income may be more difficult since disability is a costly affliction in terms of medical care and specialized treatment. And for nutrition services, disabled children get less help than most other groups, whereas for income services they are among the groups who receive high support. Also, transportation services are probably more crucial for meeting essential needs of the disabled than for the poor, and higher support rankings went to the disabled than to the poor.

The "Deserving" and the "Undeserving"

One of the earliest distinctions in the history of public assistance was that between "the deserving" and "the undeserving." This was one of the major concepts in the Elizabethan Poor Law of 1601 (Stein, 1971: 47) and it continues to be used in decisions about who gets help today, according to several commentators (Macarov, 1978). The assumption is that the "deserving" poor can be separated from the undeserving according to whether or not the individual caused his own plight. According to Stein (1971), the deserving poor are those who are dependent through no fault of their own (1971: 47). In fact, the first question that Charity Organization Society workers asked themselves in the late 1900s and early twentieth century to determine who should be helped was: "What is the cause of the distress?" (Woodroffe, 1961: 36). And if the person caused his or her own plight, he or she was considered "undeserving" and denied aid.

Our findings offer some empirical basis for examining this age old distinction. If one reexamines Figures 5.1 b and d, it can be seen that the seven welfare groups are similarly ranked on the measures of deservingness and responsibility for condition. Thus, those groups that are seen as least responsible for their condition are ranked as high in deservingness. The second point to note is that the groups seen as most deserving and least responsible are the same groups that were considered to be most deserving under thhe old deserving-undeserving dichotomy, i.e., elderly, physically disabled, and children.

The next question to be asked is whether support is given according to these patterns of deservingness and responsibility for condition. The answer is "not always." The pattern of support varies from service to service. Respondents do not make each support decision for each service based on notions in the abstract of fault and deservingness. And though poor adults of working age are considered least deserving and most responsible for their plight in the abstract, they do not always get supported least. In fact for educational services they get more support than any other group.

Why is this? We think it may be because the general public will support groups for services if (1) the service can help the group achieve independence, as educational services could help poor adults but not necessarily help elderly persons; and (2) if the group has no alternative source of aid. In the latter connection, one should note that, unlike disabled adults of all ages, who often do not have other relatives to look after them, disabled children—who are usually thought to have parents to help them—are much less helped.

As with many sharp distinctions, the deserving-undeserving dichotomy is too simplistic to be useful. Though respondents are able to make decisions in the abstract of who they consider deserving, they do not reflexively apply this conception to decisions about how much support to give for any particular service. The question the Chicago public seems to be asking is: "deserving of what?" rahter than "are they deserving?"

MORE GENERAL ISSUES

The preceding discussion was concerned with reporting findings and discussing their separate implications for a number of theoretical and policy issues. We want now to take a further step back from the data and discuss their implication for two more general issues: consulting the public about funding priorities and interpreting the recent "taxpayers' revolt."

Consulting the Public About Funding Priorities

The research presented in this book goes some way toward dispelling two widely held myths about consulting the public about welfare matters. One is that the public is undiscriminating in its support, basing preferences on stereotypes or on the attractiveness of welfare groups rather than on their unique needs and the ability to meet these needs from sources other than public funds. The second is that public support is so dependent on a self-interest which varies from segment to segment that no public opinion about support exists. According to this view, the public is fragmented, and consulting it about preferences may widen differences and make political action more, rather than less, difficult.

We are prepared to assume that the major actors who determine the funding priorities for welfare groups do so in a context that takes account of the actors' perceptions of what the public will countenance and what they think the public's preference orderings are. How much weight such perceptions have—in light of the many other causal factors that determine decisions—is not at all clear, and is not the central issue here. The central issue is whether public opinion is considered at all. If we are prepared to believe that it is considered, then we have to wonder, first, how accurate are the perceptions, and second, at what level of differentiation are they formulated.

The prevalence of questions in polling studies about "welfare" in general leads us to suggest that most data-based thinking about support is global and may have an inappropriate referent. That is, for poll respondents, the referent for welfare may be poor persons of working age rather than any one of the many other types of welfare recipients who can be found. Unfortunately, there is a dearth of truly comparative studies of support for different welfare groups, at least in the published literature. This dearth leads us to suspect that the impression left by responses to general items dealing with welfare can hardly have been refuted by data. It also leads us to suspect that the comparative judgments of decision influencers may have been molded by personal impressions and social stereotypes rather than by hard-headed reality testing. Most decision influencers would probably easily be able to claim that the public supports the disabled more than the poor, and elderly adults and children more than persons of working age. However, it is less likely that decision influencers would be as confident or as accurate about the support for the disabled or poor vs. disaster victims, or for the elderly vs. children, or for disabled adults under 65 vs. the elderly poor, etc. If our assumptions are correct, then comparative information about public opinion is being used to an unknown extent in decision-making, and it is hardly likely that this information is accurate, particularly in specifics.

It is also unlikely that the information considered by decision-makers is finely differentiated. We understand this in two senses: at the subgroup level we examined—i.e. age groups *within* the disabled and poor—or at the level of relating different services to different groups. Are the persons responsible for providing nutritional services mindful of how the public might react to providing these services to disabled children as opposed to disabled adults, whether elderly or not? Are the persons responsible for public education mindful, in their advocacy of "life-long learning," that the public may not look kindly at significant sums being spent from the public purse for the elderly poor as opposed to poor adults? Our guess is that global estimates of differences in public support are not accurate, and may, in fact, be rather inaccurate.

The case for increased consultation of the general public
does not rest solely on the possibility that inaccurate and
undifferentiated perceptions of differences in support are
already being used as part of the input into decision-making.
A normative case can also be made. We live in a political
democracy where the public purse is taking over more and
more of the welfare functions that were formerly part of the
responsibility of families, churches, and other voluntary organizations. To consult the public on how its money is spent
would seem reasonable, all the more so since we know that
the public does not weigh its parochial self-interests very
heavily in the preferences it has. Moreover, it does not react
to the plight of various welfare groups in an undifferentiated
manner that uncritically supports some groups over others
and that is insensitive to the unique needs of particular
groups.

These last points are important. The argument could be
made that it is unwise to consult the public on allocative
priorities because this reduces policy-making to a popularity
contest in which the least popular might be victimized even
more because of their lack of popularity. Though some
groups are in general preferred more than others, this preference is far from universal and cannot be described as the
uncritical popularity of some groups over others. Instead,
support depends on the relationship of groups and services,
and is probably contingent on public perceptions of the
extent of need, the availability of help from other sources,
and the likelihood that the help will create independence,
either physical or financial. A further point also needs to be
made when we consider the popularity argument. Most advocates of increased public consultation would, we surmise, not
be so naive as to believe that allocative decisions *could* ever
be based solely on public preferences. Other factors, ranging
from interest group politics to chance, play important roles
in molding decisions. We also surmise that most of the
advocates would abjure the position that allocative decisions

should be based solely on public preferences. Instead, we might presume that their argument would only be that the public should be consulted, and in a sophisticated and differentiated manner.

Consulting the public about comparative preferences may have unplanned negative side-effects. In particular, it might increase the saliency of competition between social welfare groups, thereby exacerbating conflicts or creating conflicts where none previously seemed to exist. This point has some validity. Much of the current public funding for social welfare groups comes from categorical funds that are targeted at specific demographic groups that are presumed to have particular needs. For instance, in education, funds are set aside for both disabled and poor children; in the nutrition area, funds are set aside for the elderly disabled and poor children of school age. The prevalence of categorical funding seems, at first glance, to imply an absence of competition *between* the groups we studied, and seems rather to imply only a competition *within* the groups. However, this impression is erroneous in some absolute sense, for somewhere decisions have to be made about how much is to be allocated to each category. Here, the relevant groups have interests that are in conflict. Moreover, with some programs—like the Title XX we discussed in Chapter 1—conflict between the social welfare groups is built into the process whereby funds are allocated at the state level. And finally, we should not forget that the number of persons in need is likely to increase at a faster rate in the future than is the size of the financial pie that will be devoted to payments for social services, broadly conceived. This alone suggests that conflicts will probably be exacerbated in the future and that allocative decisions will have to be made with an even greater consciousness of who will be helped and hurt by distributional decisions.

These last points indicate the illusory nature of the present appearance of a lack of conflict, and they also indicate that conflicts may become more salient in the future. But why should we make such conflicts more salient at the present time both by forcing comparisons between welfare groups and then publicizing the findings? To this our principal answer is: The conflicts exist, and because they may become more acute in the future, it is probably advantageous to prepare the public and some decision-makers for the difficult decisions that will probably have to be faced soon, even if preparing them inadvertently advances the day when conflicts between the groups are more salient and demand more immediate attention. Little of an important and enduring nature is promoted by pretending that the interests of one welfare group do not depend to some degree on another's or by denying that the public voice deserves being heard as one input into political debates about allocative priorities.

The Taxpayers' Revolt

In the late 1970s much was made in the media about a taxpayers' revolt, the most visible symbol of which was probably Proposition 13 that was passed in California in 1978. The data reported in this book were not collected for the express purpose of probing issues relating to the taxpayers' revolt. But they are germane to this issue in several ways that are discussed below.

The first point to be made is that, in general, the support for social welfare groups was strongest among the lower-income groups, who, it could be argued, pay less taxes in an absolute sense. This suggests that taxpayers, if not in revolt, are at least relatively more reluctant to offer support than other groups.

Moreover, it should be noted that support was surprisingly low for some particular combinations of services and groups, at least when compared to the level of support offered these groups for other services. Salient examples of this include public education for the elderly and nutritional services for disabled children. We infer from this that the public considers some services to be inappropriate for some groups, and would not take kindly to seeing funds disbursed for such purposes. In a related vein, it is worth noting that the public does not generally support groups like the poor of working age, so that if it is believed that this one group consumes a great deal of tax resources or captures a great deal of public attention, then feelings about this one group might influence more general feelings about services for all welfare groups and result in what appears to be a tax revolt.

Close examination of our data reveals, however, that when the general public in Chicago was asked about specific services for specific groups, support was often high. Indeed, measures of reported willingness to have one's taxes stay the same or *increased* to support some groups showed that for many services and groups more persons were against a decrease than for it; and that among those against a decrease, a significant percentage was in favor of an increase rather than in favor of no increase.

It is probably an oversimplification to say that the American public wants taxes decreased and services cut. There may well be a willingness to agree to such statements under conditions where (a) budget surpluses exist and are growing; (b) large sums of money are wasted or disbursed under false pretenses or in a haphazard, ineffective manner; and (c) when specific services are not seen as meeting the basic needs of target groups, or are not seen as promoting their physical or financial independence. Where such conditions are not present and where programs are seen as relevant to meeting basic needs and promoting independence, taxpayers may not be in revolt. Indeed, they may even be willing to see their taxes increased slightly. Our guess, based on the data presented in Chapters 3 through 5, is that taxpayers are more likely to be reacting angrily to pointless spending that fails to promote the well-being of persons in need than they are to careful spending that is geared to the unique needs of individuals in particular plights.

The survey research techniques we used provide a convenient vehicle for monitoring perceptions of the services that the public is likely to support. Perhaps more important than this is that ongoing surveys which ask about particular services for particular groups may help in some small way to present the issue of a taxpayers' revolt in a more differentiated and accurate way than is the case when headlines stress taxpayers refusing to support global issues for tax spending rather than specific issues. A heightened sense of the public's consciousness and discernment about the welfare arena might go a long way toward restating just what the taxpayers are revolting against, what they are prepared to see supported as before, and what they would like to see funded more heavily. Our data certainly suggest that the public is not, willy-nilly, against public spending in the welfare domain.

APPENDIX 1
THE QUESTIONNAIRE

```
┌─────────────┐
│  SCREENER   │
└─────────────┘
```

INTRODUCTION:

Hello, I'm from the National Opinion Research Center. We are interested
in talking to people of different ages and incomes to find out what the
public thinks the government in Washington should do to help certain
groups of people. My assignment is to interview households where the·
head of household and spouse earn (REFER TO INCOME CATEGORIES IN S.1).

IF R SEEMS RELUCTANT:

Your responses are voluntary, private and entirely confidential. No
information about any individual is ever given to anyone. Your answers
are added to those of other people in the form of statistics.

S.1.   Does the head of this household and spouse have a combined income of:

     A.   IF BLACK HOUSEHOLD

          AND HIGH INCOME AREA, ASK:
          $15,000 or more a year?

          AND MIDDLE INCOME AREA, ASK:
          between $8,000 and $15,000 a year?

          AND LOW INCOME AREA, ASK:
          $8,000 or less a year?

     B.   IF WHITE HOUSEHOLD

          AND HIGH INCOME AREA, ASK:
          $20,000 or more a year?

          AND MIDDLE INCOME AREA, ASK:
          between $10,000·and $20,000 a year?

          AND LOW INCOME AREA, ASK:
          $10,000 or less a year?

```
┌──────────────────────────────────────────┐
│ IF "NO" TO S.1, TERMINATE THE INTERVIEW   │
└──────────────────────────────────────────┘
```

S.2.   Is there any member of this household who is (REFER TO ASSIGNMENT SHEET FOR
      AGE AND SEX QUOTAS TO BE FILLED)?

      IF SCREENER RESPONDENT MEETS YOUR QUOTA, GO TO PAGE 2.

      IF SCREENER RESPONDENT DOES NOT MEET YOUR QUOTA, BUT SOMEONE IN THE
      HOUSEHOLD DOES, ASK S.3.

```
        ┌──────────────────────────────────────────────┐
        │ IF NO ONE MEETS QUOTA, TERMINATE THE INTERVIEW │
        └──────────────────────────────────────────────┘
```

S.3.   (Is that person/Are any of those persons) home?

      IF "YES," ASK TO SPEAK WITH THE PERSON (OR ONE OF THE PERSONS) NOW.

      IF NOT HOME, ASK THE SCREENER RESPONDENT FOR THE BEST TIME TO
      REACH THE PERSON(S) WHO MEETS THE QUOTA.

Now I'd like to ask a few background questions.

Time Started [:   ] AM / PM

A. To start, how many people live in this household? . . ... [ ][ ]   15-16/

B. Let's start with you. Your first name will do.
    (ENTER NAME ON LINE 01, BELOW.)

C. And the other members of this household--what are their names? Let's begin with
    everyone related to you.   (ENTER FIRST NAMES IN TABLE BELOW.)

D. Are there other people living here who are not related to you?
    (ENTER NAMES IN TABLE BELOW.)

E. I have listed (READ NAMES IN ORDER). Is there anyone else staying here now,
    such as a friend, relative, or roomer who has been living here for at least
    six months? IF YES, ENTER NAME BELOW. IF NO, CHECK HERE [ ] .

F. Have I missed anyone who usually lives here six months or more of the year but who
    is now away from home? IF YES, LIST BELOW. IF NO, CHECK HERE [ ] .

G. Do any of the people you have told me about have a home anywhere else where
    they live six or more months of the year? IF YES, CROSS OFF LIST. IF NO,
    CHECK HERE [ ] .

	H. ASK H-K FOR EACH PERSON AS APPROPRIATE.	H. What is (PERSON)'s relation-ship to you?	I. CODE SEX (ASK IF NOT OB-VIOUS) M | F	J. How old (were you/was PERSON) on (your/his/her) last birthday?	K. IF 16 YEARS OR OLDER, ASK: (Are you/Is PERSON) now married, widowed, divorced or annulled, separated, or (have you/has he/she) never been married? (IF REPORTED AS LIVING TOGETHER BUT NOT FORMALLY MARRIED, CODE "INFORMAL.") Marr. | Wid. | Div.. Annul. | Sep. | Never Marr. | In-formal
			17/	18-19	20/
01		RESPONDENT	1 2		3 4 5 6 7 8
02			1 2		3 4 5 6 7 8
03			1 2		3 4 5 6 7 8
04			1 2		3 4 5 6 7 8
05			1 2		3 4 5 6 7 8
06			1 2		3 4 5 6 7 8
07			1 2		3 4 5 6 7 8
08			1 2		3 4 5 6 7 8
09			1 2		3 4 5 6 7 8
10			1 2		3 4 5 6 7 8

1. Altogether, how many children do you have?   ENTER # CHILDREN: _____   21/

2. ASK FOR EACH PARENT AND CODE IN APPROPRIATE COLUMN:
    Is your (mother/father) living?

	Mother 22/	Father 23/
Yes . . (ASK A)	1	1
No	2	2
Don't know	3	3
Not applicable	4	4

A. IF YES: About how old is (she/he)?

Mother's age: _____   24-25/

Father's age: _____   26-27/

3.

	A. What is the last grade you completed in school? (RESPONDENT)	B. How about your (husband/wife)? (SPOUSE, IF MARRIED)
	28-29/	30-31/
8th grade or less	01	01
1-3 years of high school	02	02
High school graduate	03	03
1-3 years of college	04	04
Business or trade school	05	05
College graduate	06	06
Some graduate school	07	07
Law school graduate, M.A. degree.	08	08
Ph.D. degree	09	09
M.D. degree	10	10
Now a college student	11	11
NA	12	12

---

4. What is the highest grade of school your (mother/MOTHER SUBSTITUTE) completed?

USE CODE CATEGORIES FROM Q. 3: ☐☐   32-33/

Don't know 98

---

5. What is the highest grade of school your (father/FATHER SUBSTITUTE) completed?

USE CODE CATEGORIES FROM Q. 3: ☐☐   34-35/

Don't know 98

CIRCLE VIGNETTE USED: REPLICATION   1   2

RESPONDENT 1 2 3 4 5 6 7 8

6. Now, I'm going to read descriptions of 8 people in 8 different situations. After each description, I'll be asking you a few questions about the person in the story. They might all sound similar at first, but they are all somewhat different so you'll probably want to listen carefully. Some you might have great sympathy with, some you might not. Some you might think the government should finance services for, some you might not. Of course, there are no right or wrong answers, only your opinions.

Here's the first one. READ FIRST VIGNETTE AND ASK (1) & (2).

(1) Do you have any sympathy for (VIGNETTE CHARACTER'S NAME) and the situation he is in? CIRCLE ANSWER CODE IN BOX BELOW.

	36/	37/	38/	39/	40/	41/	42/	43/
VIGNETTE CHARACTER →	A	B	C	D	E	F	G	H
Yes	1	1	1	1	1	1	1	1
No	2	2	2	2	2	2	2	2
Don't know	9	9	9	9	9	9	9	9

(2) Do you think it's important to have services financed by the federal government to help people in situations like (VIGNETTE CHARACTER'S NAME) is in? CIRCLE ANSWER CODE IN BOX BELOW.

	44/	45/	46/	47/	48/	49/	50/	51/
VIGNETTE CHARACTER →	A	B	C	D	E	F	G	H
Yes [ASK (3)-(5)]	1	1	1	1	1	1	1	1
No [GO TO NEXT VIGNETTE]	2	2	2	2	2	2	2	2
Don't know	9	9	9	9	9	9	9	9

6. (Continued)

IF YES TO (2), ASK (3)-(5):

(3) There are a number of things which people can do to support service programs
     to help people in conditions like (VIGNETTE CHARACTER'S NAME). One might
     be to sign a petition or write a letter to someone who is responsible
     for such programs.

     Would you sign a petition or write a letter to someone in government
     supporting such programs? CIRCLE ANSWER CODE IN BOX BELOW.

	52/	53/	54/	55/	56/	57/	58/	59/
VIGNETTE CHARACTER →	A	B	C	D	E	F	G	H
Yes, probably	1	1	1	1	1	1	1	1
No, probably not	2	2	2	2	2	2	2	2
Don't know	9	9	9	9	9	9	9	9

(4) Another way might be to attend a local public meeting to demonstrate
     support for programs to help people in conditions like (VIGNETTE
     CHARACTER'S NAME) is in. Would you attend such a meeting?
     CIRCLE ANSWER CODE IN BOX BELOW.

	60/	61/	62/	63/	64/	65/	66/	67/
VIGNETTE CHARACTER →	A	B	C	D	E	F	G	H
Yes, probably	1	1	1	1	1	1	1	1
No, probably not	2	2	2	2	2	2	2	2
Don't know	9	9	9	9	9	9	9	9

(5) Suppose that services for people like (VIGNETTE CHARACTER'S NAME) couldn't
     be supplied unless taxes were raised. Would you be willing to pay slightly
     higher taxes to support programs to help people like him?
     CIRCLE ANSWER CODE IN BOX BELOW.

	68/	69/	70/	71/	72/	73/	74/	75/
VIGNETTE CHARACTER →	A	B	C	D	E	F	G	H
Yes	1	1	1	1	1	1	1	1
No	2	2	2	2	2	2	2	2
Don't know	9	9	9	9	9	9	9	9

INTERVIEWER INSTRUCTION: GO TO NEXT VIGNETTE. ASK APPROPRIATE QUESTIONS
                          AND CONTINUE UNTIL ALL 8 VIGNETTES ARE READ.

                                                        76-77/
                                                        78-79/
                                                         80/1

BEGIN DECK 2

7. We're interested in finding out some of your opinions about seven different groups
   of people. They are:

   HAND
CARD
A

   1) People <u>over 65</u> who are <u>poor</u>
   2) People <u>over 65</u> who are <u>physically disabled</u> or <u>handicapped</u>
   3) <u>Children</u> who are <u>disabled</u>
   4) <u>Children</u> from <u>poor</u> families
   5) <u>Victims</u> of <u>natural disasters</u>, such as floods or tornadoes
   6) <u>Poor</u> people <u>under 65</u>
   and 7) <u>Physically disabled</u> people <u>under 65</u>.

   Here is a picture of a ladder. Suppose we say that the top of the ladder

   HAND
PICTURE
OF
LADDER
   (INTERVIEWER POINTS) represents the best possible life and the
   bottom (POINTING) represents the worst possible life.

ENTER
STEP #:

```
 10    Best
       Possible
  9    Life
  8
  7
  6
  5
  4
  3
  2
  1    Worst
       Possible
  0    Life
```

A. Where on the ladder (MOVING FINGER RAPIDLY
   UP AND DOWN LADDER) do you think people over 65
   who are poor stand at the present time?
   IF CLARIFICATION IS NEEDED, INTERVIEWER SAYS:
   That is, people over 65 who are poor <u>as a group</u>.
   On the average, where do you think they stand? . ____   4-5/

   (1) Where do you think poor elderly people
       stood 5 years ago? . . . . ____   6-7/

B. Where do you think elderly people who are
   physically disabled stand on the ladder <u>now</u>? . . . ____   8-9/

   (1) Where do you think they stood 5 years ago? . ____   10-11/

C. Where do you think poor adults under 65 stand
   on the ladder <u>now</u>? . . . . ____   12-13/

   (1) What about 5 years ago? . . . . ____   14-15/

D. Where do you think physically disabled adults
   under 65 stand on the ladder <u>now</u>? . . . . ____   16-17/

   (1) What about 5 years ago? . . . . ____   18-19/

E. Where do you think poor children stand on the
   ladder <u>now</u>? . . . . ____   20-21/

   (1) What about 5 years ago? . . . . ____   22-23/

F. Where do you think physically disabled children
   stand on the ladder <u>now</u>? . . . . ____   24-25/

   (1) What about 5 years ago? . . . . ____   26-27/

G. Where on the ladder do you feel you personally
   stand at the <u>present</u> time? . . . . ____   28-29/

   (1) Where on the ladder would you say you stood
       5 years ago? . . . . ____   30-31/

   (2) And where do you think you will be on the
       ladder 5 years from now? . . . . ____   32-33/

8. There are a number of services financed by the federal government to provide for
    some of the needs of each of these seven groups--for example, programs that
    provide money, food or medical care. Some people feel there should be even _more_
    services for particular groups; other people feel there should be fewer programs.
    And other people, of course, have opinions somewhere in between.

    We'd like to know how _you_ feel about services financed by the federal
    government for the groups we've mentioned. First, let's consider people
    over 65 who are _poor_.

  If you feel that public programs and services for the
            elderly poor should be greatly increased, pick box 7.
            If you think services should be greatly reduced, pick
            box 1. If you feel public programs should stay at the
            same level, pick box number 4. What box best describes
            your opinions? ENTER NUMBER ON LINE BELOW AND CONTINUE
            ASKING B-G.

                              "SERVICES SCALE"

          Decrease Number   Increase Number of
       of Public Programs   1 2 3 4 5 6 7   Public Programs

                                      Keep
                                   Same Level

                                                            ENTER
                                                            BOX #
                                                              ↓
    IF NECESSARY, REPEAT A; OTHERWISE, ENTER # ON LINE & ASK B.

    A. People over 65 who are _poor_ ?   _____   34/

    B. What box best describes your opinion about public
        programs for _people over 65_ who are _physically disabled_?   _____   35/

    C. Next, how about public programs for _handicapped children_?   _____   36/

    D. Now what about _children_ in _poor families_?   _____   37/

    E. What about public programs for victims of
        natural disasters?   _____   38/

    F. Next, what about public services for _poor adults_ who
        are _under 65_?   _____   39/

    G. Finally, how about adults _under 65_ who are _physically
        handicapped_?   _____   40/

9. Now I would like to discuss with you some <u>specific</u> programs and services for each of the seven groups.

   First, let's talk about food programs.

   A service provided in some places for people over 65 who are handicapped is called "Meals-on-Wheels." Once a day, nutritious meals are brought to elderly people who cannot cook for themselves. Some people think that this program should be expanded to reach <u>more</u> elderly, disabled people. Others think that this program is not very important and should be cut back. How do you feel--should other programs be cut back to expand the Meals-on-Wheels program for the elderly, should the Meals-on-Wheels program for the elderly be cut back to give more attention to other public needs, or are you pretty much satisfied with the way things are?

Cut back other programs to expand Meals-on-Wheels . . . . . . (ASK A) . . 1		41/
Cut back Meals-on-Wheels . . . . (ASK B) . . 2		
Satisfied . . . . (GO TO Q. 10) . 3		
Expand Meals-on-Wheels but don't cut back on anything . . . . . (ASK C & D) . . 4		

   A. How strongly do you feel that other programs should be cut in order to expand the Meals-on-Wheels program for the elderly--would you say very strongly, fairly strongly, or not too strongly?

Very strongly . . . (ASK C & D) . . . 1		42/
Fairly strongly . . (ASK C & D) . . . 2		
Not too strongly . . (ASK C & D) . . . 3		

   B. How strongly do you feel that the Meals-on-Wheels program for the elderly should be cut back to give more attention to other public needs, would you say very strongly, fairly strongly, or not too strongly?

Very strongly . . . (ASK C) . . 1		43/
Fairly strongly . . (ASK C) . . 2		
Not too strongly . (ASK C) . . 3		

   C. Do you feel strongly enough about your opinion that you would be willing to sign a petition or write a letter to someone in government stating your point of view on this program? READ ANSWER CATEGORIES.

Definitely yes 1		44/
Probably yes 2		
Probably no 3		
Definitely no 4		
DO NOT READ: Don't know 9		

   D. Suppose it were necessary to raise taxes in order to be able to enlarge this program to serve more people. <u>About</u> how much more would you be willing to pay? Would you be willing to pay no more in taxes, $1.00 more for every $100.00 in taxes you already pay, $3.00 more for every $100.00 in taxes you already pay, or $5.00 more for every $100.00 in taxes?

No more 1		45/
$1.00 more 2		
$3.00 more 3		
$5.00 more 4		
Don't know 9		

10. We've just talked about Meals-on-Wheels for elderly people who can't cook for
     themselves. Some physically <u>disabled</u> people who are <u>under 65</u> are so handicapped
     that they can't prepare meals either.

     How do you feel about the Meals-on-Wheels program for disabled people under 65?
     Should other programs be cut back to expand the Meals-on-Wheels program for
     disabled people under 65, should the Meals-on-Wheels program for disabled under
     65 be cut back to give more attention to other public needs, or are you pretty
     much satisfied with the way things are now?

```
                        Cut back other programs . . (ASK A) . . . . 1        46/
                        Cut back Meals-on-Wheels  . (ASK B) . . . . 2
                        Satisfied  . . . . . . (GO TO Q. 11) . . . 3
                        Expand but don't cut back . (ASK C & D) . . 4
```

A. How strongly do you feel that other programs should be cut back in order
    to expand the Meals-on-Wheels program for disabled people under 65--would
    you say very strongly, fairly strongly, or not too strongly?

```
                        Very strongly .  (ASK C & D) . . 1        47/
                        Fairly strongly .(ASK C & D) . . 2
                        Not too strongly.(ASK C & D) . . 3
```

B. How strongly do you feel that the Meals-on-Wheels program for disabled
    people under 65 should be cut back to give more attention to other public
    needs--would you say very strongly, fairly strongly, or not too strongly?

```
                        Very strongly . . . (ASK C)  . . 1        48/
                        Fairly strongly . . (ASK C)  . . 2
                        Not too strongly  . (ASK C)  . . 3
```

C. Would you sign a petition or write a letter to someone in government
    stating your point of view on this program? READ ANSWER CATEGORIES.

```
                        Definitely yes . . . . . . . . 1        49/
                        Probably yes . . . . . . . . . 2
                        Probably no  . . . . . . . . . 3
                        Definitely no  . . . . . . . . 4
        DO NOT READ: Don't know . . . . . . . . . . 9
```

D. <u>INTERVIEWER</u>: USE ONLY IF   ⌈ If it were necessary to raise taxes in order
    ASKING TAX QUESTION FOR THE   ⟨ to enlarge this program, about how much
    FIRST TIME OR IF NECESSARY   ⌊ more taxes would you be willing to pay?
    TO REFRESH R'S MEMORY.

    Would you be willing to pay no more in taxes, $1.00 more for every $100.00
    in taxes you already pay, $3.00 more for every $100.00 in taxes you already
    pay, or $5.00 more for every $100.00 in taxes?

```
                        No more . . . . . . . . . . . 1        50/
                        $1.00 more  . . . . . . . . . 2
                        $3.00 more . . . . . . . . . . 3
                        $5.00 more . . . . . . . . . . 4
                        Don't know . . . . . . . . . 9
```

.1. The Food Stamp Program is a program to help poor people buy food because they
     cannot otherwise get an adequate diet. Some people feel this is a necessary
     program for poor people under 65 and should be expanded. Other people feel that
     this program should be cut back.

     How do you feel about the Food Stamp Program? Should other programs be cut
     back to expand the Food Stamp Program, should the Food Stamp Program be cut back
     to give more attention to other public needs, or are you pretty much satisfied
     with the way things are now?

                    Cut back other programs . . . . (ASK A) . . 1   51/
                    Cut back the Food Stamp Program (ASK B) . . 2
                    Satisfied . . . . (GO TO Q. 12) . . . 3
                    Expand but don't cut back . (ASK C & D) . . 4

A.   How strongly do you feel that other programs should be cut back in order
     to expand the Food Stamp Program for poor people under 65--would you say
     very strongly, fairly strongly, or not too strongly?

                    Very strongly . (ASK C & D) . . 1   52/
                    Fairly strongly .(ASK C & D) . . 2
                    Not too strongly.(ASK C & D) . . 3

B.   How strongly do you feel that the Food Stamp Program for poor people
     under 65 should be cut back to give more attention to other public
     needs--would you say very strongly, fairly strongly, or not too strongly?

                    Very strongly . . . (ASK C) . . 1   53/
                    Fairly strongly . . (ASK C) . . 2
                    Not too strongly . (ASK C) . . 3

C.   Would you sign a petition or write a letter to someone in government
     stating your point of view on this program? READ ANSWER CATEGORIES.
                    Definitely yes 1   54/
                    Probably yes 2
                    Probably no 3
                    Definitely no 4
          DO NOT READ: Don't know 9

D.   (INTERVIEWER: USE TAX QUESTION INTRODUCTION ONLY IF NECESSARY.)

     To support the Food Stamp Program for poor people under 65, we'd like to
     know _about_ how much more you'd be willing to pay in taxes, if any.
     Would you be willing to pay no more in taxes, $1.00 more for every $100.00
     in taxes you already pay, $3.00 more for every $100.00 in taxes you already
     pay, or $5.00 more for every $100.00 in taxes?

                    No more 1   55/
                    $1.00 more 2
                    $3.00 more 3
                    $5.00 more 4
                    Don't know 9

12. I would now like to talk with you about the School Lunch Program. Lunches are
     provided free or at reduced costs to children whose parents are unable to pay
     the full price. Some people think this is an important program, while other
     people feel it is not a very important program.

     How do you feel about the School Lunch Program for poor children? Should other
     programs be cut back to expand the School Lunch Program, should the School Lunch
     Program be cut back to give more attention to other public needs, or are you
     pretty much satisfied with the way things are now?

                     Cut back other programs . . . . .(ASK A) . . . 1
                     Cut back the School Lunch Program (ASK B) . . . 2   56/
                     Satisfied . . . . (GO TO Q. 13) . . 3
                     Expand but don't cut back . (ASK C & D) . . . 4

  A. How strongly do you feel that other programs should be cut back in order
      to expand the School Lunch Program--would you say very strongly,
      fairly strongly, or not too strongly?

                          Very strongly . (ASK C & D) . . 1   57/
                          Fairly strongly .(ASK C & D) . . 2
                          Not too strongly.(ASK C & D) . . 3

  B. How strongly do you feel that the School Lunch Program should be cut back
      to give more attention to other public needs--would you say very strongly,
      fairly strongly, or not too strongly?

                          Very strongly . . . (ASK C) . . 1   58/
                          Fairly strongly . . (ASK C) . . 2
                          Not too strongly . (ASK C) . . 3

  C. Would you sign a petition or write a letter to someone in government
      stating your point of view on this program?   READ ANSWER CATEGORIES.

                          Definitely yes 1   59/
                          Probably yes 2
                          Probably no 3
                          Definitely no 4
             DO NOT READ: Don't know 9

  D. (INTERVIEWER: USE TAX QUESTION INTRODUCTION ONLY IF NECESSARY.)

      To support the School Lunch Program for poor children, we'd like to
      know about how much more you'd be willing to pay in taxes, if any.
      Would you be willing to pay no more in taxes, $1.00 more for every $100.00
      in taxes you already pay, $3.00 more for every $100.00 in taxes you already
      pay, or $5.00 more for every $100.00 in taxes?

                          No more 1   60/
                          $1.00 more 2
                          $3.00 more 3
                          $5.00 more 4
                          Don't know 9

13. In a very few places, school lunches are provided free or at reduced costs
     to physically disabled children, no matter what their parent's income. A
     variety of opinions exist about the importance of such a program.

     How do you feel about a School Lunch Program for disabled children? Should
     other programs be cut back to expand the School Lunch Program for disabled
     children, should the School Lunch Program for disabled children be cut back
     to give more attention to other public needs, or are you pretty much satisfied
     with the way things are now?

                    Cut back other programs . . . . . (ASK A) . . 1
                    Cut back the School Lunch Program . (ASK B) . . 2   61/
                    Satisfied . . . . (GO TO Q. 14) . 3
                    Expand but don't cut back . . (ASK C & D) . . 4

A.   How strongly do you feel that other programs should be cut back in order
     to expand the School Lunch Program for disabled children--would you say
     very strongly, fairly strongly, or not too strongly?

                         Very strongly . (ASK C & D) . . 1   62/

                         Fairly strongly .(ASK C & D) . . 2

                         Not too strongly.(ASK C & D) . . 3

B.   How strongly do you feel that the School Lunch Program for disabled children
     should be cut back to give more attention to other public needs--would you
     say very strongly, fairly strongly, or not too strongly?

                         Very strongly . . . (ASK C) . . 1   63/

                         Fairly strongly . . (ASK C) . . 2

                         Not too strongly . (ASK C) . . 3

C.   Would you sign a petition or write a letter to someone in government
     stating your point of view on this program?   READ ANSWER CATEGORIES.
                         Definitely yes 1   64/
                         Probably yes 2
                         Probably no 3
                         Definitely no 4
               DO NOT READ: Don't know 9

D.   (INTERVIEWER: USE TAX QUESTION INTRODUCTION ONLY IF NECESSARY.)

     To support the School Lunch Program for physically disabled children, we'd like
     to know about how much more you'd be willing to pay in taxes, if any.
     Would you be willing to pay no more in taxes, $1.00 more for every $100.00
     in taxes you already pay, $3.00 more for every $100.00 in taxes you already
     pay, or $5.00 more for every $100.00 in taxes?

                         No more 1   65/

                         $1.00 more 2

                         $3.00 more 3

                         $5.00 more 4

                         Don't know 9

14. How about a Food Stamp Program for people over 65 who are poor and can't buy
    adequate food. Some people feel the Food Stamp Program should be enlarged
    especially for senior citizens who are poor. Others disagree.

    How do you feel about the Food Stamp Program for people over 65 who are poor?
    Should other programs be cut back to expand the Food Stamp Program for the elderly
    poor, should the Food Stamp Program for the elderly poor be cut back to give more
    attention to other public needs, or are you pretty much satisfied with the way
    things are now?

                    Cut back other programs . . . . . (ASK A) . 1
                    Cut back Food Stamp Program . . . . (ASK B) . 2   66/
                    Satisfied . . . . (GO TO Q. 15). 3
                    Expand but don't cut back . . . . (ASK C & D). 4

A. How strongly do you feel that other programs should be cut back in order
    to expand the Food Stamp Program for the elderly poor--would you say
    very strongly, fairly strongly, or not too strongly?

                    Very strongly . (ASK C & D) . . 1   67/
                    Fairly strongly .(ASK C & D) . . 2
                    Not too strongly.(ASK C & D) . . 3

B. How strongly do you feel that the Food Stamp Program for the elderly poor
    should be cut back to give more attention to other public needs--would
    you say very strongly, fairly strongly, or not too strongly?

                    Very strongly . . . (ASK C) . . 1   68/
                    Fairly strongly . . (ASK C) . . 2
                    Not too strongly . (ASK C) . . 3

C. Would you sign a petition or write a letter to someone in government
    stating your point of view on this program? READ ANSWER CATEGORIES.

                    Definitely yes 1   69/
                    Probably yes 2
                    Probably no 3
                    Definitely no 4
        DO NOT READ: Don't know 9

D. (INTERVIEWER: USE TAX QUESTION INTRODUCTION ONLY IF NECESSARY.)

    To support the Food Stamp Program for the elderly poor, we'd like to know
    about how much more you'd be willing to pay in taxes, if any.
    Would you be willing to pay no more in taxes, $1.00 more for every $100.00
    in taxes you already pay, $3.00 more for every $100.00 in taxes you already
    pay, or $5.00 more for every $100.00 in taxes?

                    No more 1   70/
                    $1.00 more 2
                    $3.00 more 3
                    $5.00 more 4
                    Don't know 9

15. After natural disasters such as floods or hurricanes occur, some people feel that it is important to provide food services to the disaster victims. Other people feel that the federal government should not have this responsibility.

    How do you feel about the Food Assistance Program for disaster victims? Should other programs be cut back to expand the Food Assistance Program for disaster victims, should the Food Assistance Program for disaster victims be cut back to give more attention to other public needs, or are you pretty much satisfied with the way things are now?

Cut back other programs . . . . . (ASK A) . . 1	71/
Cut back Food Assistance Program .(ASK B) . . 2	
Satisfied . . . . (GO TO Q. 16) . 3	
Expand but don 't cut back . . . (ASK C & D). 4	

A. How strongly do you feel that other programs should be cut back in order to expand the Food Assistance Program--would you say very strongly, fairly strongly, or not too strongly?

    Very strongly . (ASK C & D) . . 1   72/

    Fairly strongly .(ASK C & D) . . 2

    Not too strongly.(ASK C & D) . . 3

B. How strongly do you feel that the Food Assistance Program should be cut back to give more attention to other public needs--would you say very strongly, fairly strongly, or not too strongly?

    Very strongly . . . (ASK C) . . 1   73/

    Fairly strongly . . (ASK C) . . 2

    Not too strongly . (ASK C) . . 3

C. Would you sign a petition or write a letter to someone in government stating your point of view on this program? READ ANSWER CATEGORIES.

Definitely yes 1	74/
Probably yes 2	
Probably no 3	
Definitely no 4	
DO NOT READ: Don't know 9	

D. (INTERVIEWER: USE TAX QUESTION INTRODUCTION ONLY IF NECESSARY.)

    To support the Food Assistance Program for disaster victims, we'd like to know about how much more you'd be willing to pay in taxes, if any. Would you be willing to pay no more in taxes, $1.00 more for every $100.00 in taxes you already pay, $3.00 more for every $100.00 in taxes you already pay, or $5.00 more for every $100.00 in taxes?

    No more 1   75/
    $1.00 more 2
    $3.00 more 3
    $5.00 more 4
    Don't know 9

CODERS ONLY:	
(Vign. Codes)	
R	76/
Inc.	77/
Sex	78/
Age	79/

    80/2

16. Now let's try to consider <u>all seven</u> programs together.   To do this, let's
    suppose that <u>you</u> are a <u>public official</u> who has to decide how much money each
    program should get.

    Let's say that the people who run these programs have come to you saying that
    they each need $100,000 extra to pay for their programs. The problem is that
    you have only $100,000 <u>total</u> to give to <u>all</u> these different programs.
    (INTERVIEWER: HAND RESPONDENT 20 $5,000 BILLS.)

    We'd like you to divide the money among all the 7 programs according to how
    important you think the individual programs are.
    (LAY OUT SPREAD CARD 1 FOR RESPONDENT TO PUT MONEY ON.)

		ENTER AMOUNT DISTRIBUTED TO EACH PROGRAM		
		# Bills	Amount	
(1)	Meals-on-Wheels for the Elderly Disabled . . .	_____	$ _____	4-5/
(2)	Food Stamp Program for Poor Elderly People . .	_____	$ _____	6-7/
(3)	Meals-on-Wheels for the Disabled People under 65	_____	$ _____	8-9/
(4)	Food Stamp Program for Poor Adults under 65 .	_____	$ _____	10-11/
(5)	School Lunch Program for Poor Children	_____	$ _____	12-13/
(6)	School Lunch Program for Disabled Children . .	_____	$ _____	14-15/
(7)	Food Assistance Program for Disaster Victims .	_____	$ _____	16-17/
	Not used	_____	$ _____	
	Should equal . . 20		$ $100,000	

INTERVIEWER NOTE:

AFTER THE RESPONDENT HAS FINISHED PLACING THE "MONEY" ON THE
SPREAD CARD, COUNT THE AMOUNT PLACED ON EACH PROGRAM AND ENTER
THAT AMOUNT ON THE APPROPRIATE LINE ABOVE. REPEAT FOR EACH
"MONEY GAME."

17. There are also a number of education-type programs that have been set up for
these seven groups. Again, just as we did before for the other programs, let's
suppose that it is your job to decide how much money should be put into these
different programs. Each program director wants $100,000 to pay for their programs.
But you have only a total of $100,000 to give to all the programs, 20 $5,000 bills.

    INTERVIEWER: HAND RESPONDENT 20 $5,000 BILLS.
    USE SPREAD CARD 2 AND POINT TO EACH PROGRAM
    AS THE PROGRAM IS DESCRIBED.

    First, let me describe briefly these programs.

		ENTER AMOUNT DISTRIBUTED TO EACH PROGRAM		
READ TO RESPONDENT:		# Bills	Amount	
(1) Information and Referral Centers for People over 65 Who Are Physically Disabled: were set up to inform them about programs which they are eligible for and to help them apply for benefits		_____	$ _____	18-19/
(2) Information and Referral Centers for People over 65 Who Are Poor: were set up to inform them about services which they are eligible for, and also show them how to apply for benefits		_____	$ _____	20-21/
(3) Rehabilitation and Job Training Programs for Physically Disabled People under 65: have been set up to help disabled people get and keep jobs .		_____	$ _____	22-23/
(4) Job Training Programs: have been set up for poor people under 65 to educate and train them so that they can get jobs		_____	$ _____	24-25/
(5) Head Start Programs for Poor Children: have been set up to give them special attention before they start school so that they will not have so much trouble later		_____	$ _____	26-27/
(6) Special Education Programs for Physically Disabled Children: have been set up to help them cope with their handicaps so that they can remain in regular schools with other children their own age		_____	$ _____	28-29/
(7) Information and Education Services for Victims of Natural Disasters, such as floods, hurricanes or tornadoes: have been set up to help natural disasters victims learn how to repair the damages done and how to apply for programs they might be eligible for		_____	$ _____	30-31/
Now place the money in the spaces by the program in the amounts you have decided to give to each.	Not used	_____	$ _____	
	Should equal . .	20	$ 100,000	

18. Transportation is a problem for some of these groups because of their special circumstances. In some places poor people are given reduced fares on public transportation and special bus transportation is provided for disabled people who can't use regular public transportation. Again, you have $100,000 to distribute among the seven groups for transportation programs. How would you divide it up? (HAND RESPONDENT 20 $5,000 BILLS. LAY OUT SPREAD CARD 3 FOR RESPONDENT TO PUT MONEY ON.)

ENTER AMOUNT
DISTRIBUTED
TO EACH PROGRAM

		# BILLS	AMOUNT	
(1)	Special bus service to physically disabled people over 65	_____	$ _____	32-33/
(2)	Half price bus fares to poor people over 65	_____	$ _____	34-35/
(3)	Special bus service for physically disabled people under 65	_____	$ _____	36-37/
(4)	Half price bus fares to poor people under 65 . . .	_____	$ _____	38-39/
(5)	Half price children's bus fares for poor children .	_____	$ _____	40-41/
(6)	Special bus service for physically disabled children	_____	$ _____	42-43/
(7)	Special transportation services for victims of natural disasters right after disasters	_____	$ _____	44-45/

IF NECESSARY:

Once again, place the money in the spaces by the programs in the amounts you have decided to give to each.

Not used . . . . .   _____ $ _____

Should equal . . .   20 $ 100,000

19. Now I'd like you to think about a proposed <u>Guaranteed Minimum Income Program</u>
for the seven groups. If an individual is not able to work full time, is not
able to work at all, or does not receive sufficient income from private means,
then he is <u>guaranteed</u> an income by the federal government. This would be the
minimum amount necessary to buy food and clothing and to pay for housing.

Again, you have $100,000 to distribute among the seven groups according to
how <u>important</u> you think income programs are for each group. How would you
divide it up? (HAND RESPONDENT 20 $5,000 BILLS. LAY OUT SPREAD CARD 4
FOR RESPONDENT TO PUT MONEY ON.)

		ENTER AMOUNT DISTRIBUTED TO EACH PROGRAM	
		# BILLS	AMOUNT
(1)	Elderly Disabled	_____	$ _____	46-47/
(2)	Elderly Poor	_____	$ _____	48-49/
(3)	Under 65 Disabled	_____	$ _____	50-51/
(4)	Under 65 Poor	_____	$ _____	52-53/

(5) Poor Children . . . . _____ $ _____ 54-55/
    (INTERVIEWER CLARIFICATION: Of course,
    this would have to go to the parents
    or the person who cares for the
    poor children.)

(6) Disabled Children . . . . _____ $ _____ 56-57/
    (INTERVIEWER CLARIfICATION: Of course,
    this would have to go to the parents
    of the children)

(7) Disaster Victims . . . . _____ $ _____ 58-59/

                                         Not used . . . _____ $ _____

                                  Should equal . 20 $ 100,000

20. Here's something a little different.

Though none of us know definitely what will happen to us in the future, most of us have a fairly good idea of how <u>likely</u> we are to face certain kinds of problems in life--such as becoming disabled or being a victim of a natural disaster. In this section, we'd like to find out how <u>likely</u> you think it is that you might have to deal with some of the problems that we've asked about before.

| HAND |
| CARD |
| C |

First let's take the problem of being a victim of a natural disaster, such as a flood or tornado. How likely is it that something like this might happen to you? Would you say practically no chance, possible but not very likely, there's a 50-50 chance, it's very likely, or you or someone close to you has already been in this situation.

Practically no chance	Possible but not likely	50-50 Chance	Very likely	Already in this situation
1	2	3	4	5

IF NECESSARY, REPEAT A; OTHERWISE ENTER # ON LINE & GO TO B.   ENTER BOX #:

·A. What is the possibility of your being a victim of a
     natural disaster, such as a flood or a tornado? . . . . _____   60/

IMPORTANT: IF R IS OBVIOUSLY VERY POOR, <u>DO NOT ASK B & C</u>.
            ENTER "5" ON PROPER LINE AND GO TO D.

B. Or being poor, how likely would you say it is that you
    could become poor? Just tell me the number of the box
    that best describes your opinion. . . . . _____   61/

C. <u>ASK ONLY IF RESPONDENT IS UNDER 65</u>:
    What is the possibility of becoming poor after you
    turn 65 or have retired? . . . . _____   62/

D. <u>ASK ONLY IF RESPONDENT DOES NOT APPEAR TO BE DISABLED
    IN ANY WAY</u>: (IF DISABLED, ENTER "5" FOR D & E AND GO TO F)
    What about becoming physically disabled in some way? . . . . _____   63/

E. <u>ASK ONLY IF RESPONDENT IS UNDER 65</u>:
    What about becoming physically disabled after retirement? . . _____   64/

INTERVIEWER: ASK F & G ONLY IF R HAS CHILDREN. (SEE Q. 1)

F. What is the possibility of one of your children, or
    grandchildren, being physically disabled? . . . . _____   65/

G. What about the possibility of one of your children, or
    grandchildren, being poor? . . . . _____   66/

21. We'd now like to learn something more about how you feel about the different groups. To do this, we'll be using sheets like these. This top sheet is only an example.

HAND R
EXAMPLE FOR
WORD PAIRS

Here's how it works. Let's say you were going to rate American Indians on one of the word pairs--deserving and undeserving. If you feel that American Indians are extremely deserving, you should put a check mark here:

Deserving __X__:_____:_____:_____:_____:_____:_____ Undeserving

OR, if you think American Indians are extremely undeserving, you should check here:

Deserving _____:_____:_____:_____:_____:_____:__X__ Undeserving

If you feel that they are quite deserving (but not extremely so), you should **put** your mark here:

Deserving _____:__X__:_____ _____ _____ _____ _____ Undeserving

INTERVIEWER:

GO THROUGH
THIS
QUICKLY
POINTING
ITEMS OUT

OR, if you think they are quite undeserving, but not extremely so, you should check here:

Deserving _____:_____:_____:_____:_____:__X__:_____ Undeserving

If you think they are only slightly deserving, then you should mark this way:

Deserving _____:_____:__X__:_____:_____:_____:_____ Undeserving

OR, if you think they are only slightly undeserving, you should check here:

Deserving _____:_____:_____:_____:__X__:_____:_____ Undeserving

Finally, mark the middle space if you feel that American Indians are neither particularly deserving or undeserving, or if you do not know, mark here:

Deserving _____:_____:_____:__X__:_____:_____:_____ Undeserving

Now, here are 7 pages of word pairs, one page for each of the 7 groups. As you see, the first page is for <u>elderly people who are poor</u>. On each page there are 4 sets of word pairs: deserving-undeserving, unpleasant-pleasant people, grateful for help-not grateful for help, hardship own fault-hardship not own fault.

Take each page, and for each word-pair, put a check mark in the space which reflects your feeling on that word-pair as it applies to the group listed at the top of the page.

22. Do you have a relative or close friend who might fit into one of the
     seven groups we have been discussing? First, (READ LIST) . . .

	Yes	No	
Someone over 65 who is poor	1	2	67/
Someone over 65 who is physically disabled or handicapped	1	2	68/
A child who is disabled	1	2	69/
Children in poor families	1	2	70/
Victims of natural disasters, such as floods or tornadoes	1	2	71/
A poor person under 65	1	2	72/
A physically disabled person under 65	1	2	73/

                                                                                    74-76/
                                                                                    77-78/

                                                                                    80/3

BEGIN DECK 4

23. I'm going to read you some statements. We'd like to know how much you
agree or disagree with them. If you agree very much, pick box +3;
if you agree on the whole, pick box +2; if you agree a little,
pick +1. If you disagree very much, pick box -3; if you
disagree on whe whole, pick -2; or if you disagree a little,
pick box -1.

HAND
CARD
D

		Agree very much +3	Agree on the whole +2	Agree a little +1	Disagree a little -1	Disagree on the whole -2	Disagree very much -3	
A.	When parents punish their children, it is almost always for good reasons.	1	2	3	4	5	6	4/
B.	People who get "lucky breaks" have usually earned their good fortune.	1	2	3	4	5	6	5/
C.	Students almost always deserve the grades they receive in school.	1	2	3	4	5	6	6/
D.	Crime doesn't pay.	1	2	3	4	5	6	7/
E.	Although evil men may hold political power for a while, in the general course of history, good wins out.	1	2	3	4	5	6	8/
F.	People who meet with misfortune often have brought it on themselves.	1	2	3	4	5	6	9/
G.	Basically, the world is a just place.	1	2	3	4	5	6	10/
H.	By and large, people deserve what they get.	1	2	3	4	5	6	11/
I.	In almost any business or profession, people who do their job well rise to the top.	1	2	3	4	5	6	12/
J.	Many people suffer through absolutely no fault of their own.	1	2	3	4	5	6	13/

24. Most people want to get certain things in life, but some people seem to
    have more than others. They may have more money, better jobs, or better
    homes. They may have better cars, TV sets, or other personal possessions.
    They may have more education or more respect. They may have more influence
    over other people.

    Is there anything you feel you are not getting a fair share of?

                            Yes . . (ASK A & B) . . . 1   14/
                            No . . (GO TO Q. 25) . . 2

    IF YES:

    A. What is it? (IF R BEGINS TO NAME MORE THAN ONE, PROBE FOR THE
                     MOST IMPORTANT ONE.)

                                                           15-16/

    B. How strongly do you feel it is unfair or unjust that you are not getting
       (WHATEVER R HAS NAMED)? Would you say you feel ... (READ CATEGORIES)

                            Extremely strong 1   17/
                            Very strong 2
                            Rather strong 3
                            Not too strong   4
              DO NOT READ: Don't know 9

───

25. Think about people who are <u>a lot like you</u>--not your family--but other people
    whose goals in life are similar to yours, or whose fate in life may be
    similar to yours. Perhaps persons who belong to your racial or nationality
    group or have the same class background as you, or who live near you or
    whoever. What group of people do you think of first? (IF R NAMES MORE THAN
    ONE GROUP, ASK WHICH GROUP OF PEOPLE HE/SHE FEELS ARE MOST LIKE R.)

    (IF R IS UNABLE TO NAME A GROUP, PROBE FURTHER WITH: Isn't there any group--
    just any group of people you feel are a lot like you, or you feel close to?)

         NAME OF GROUP: _____   18-19/

    (IF R STILL CAN'T NAME A GROUP, TRY TO FIND OUT WHETHER R CAN'T BECAUSE:)

    Is the reason you cannot name a group because you ...

              a) don't understand what the question is asking? 1   20/

              b) don't think in terms of groups, or don't feel there
                 is a group of people a lot like you? 2

              c) Or some other reason (SPECIFY) _____

                 _____ 3

                    (IF NO GROUP IS NAMED, SKIP TO Q. 27)

26. Is there anything that you <u>are</u> getting a fair share of, but that most
    (PEOPLE IN THE GROUP R HAS NAMED) <u>are not</u> getting a fair share of?

                          Yes . . . (ASK A-C) 1   21/

                          No . . . . (SKIP TO C) 2

    IF YES:

    A. What is it? (IF R BEGINS TO NAME SEVERAL, PROBE FOR THE MOST
       IMPORTANT ONE.)

                                                                   22-23/

    B. How strongly do you feel it is unfair or unjust that most (PEOPLE IN
       GROUP R HAS NAMED) are not getting a fair share of (WHATEVER R NAMED)?
       Would you say you feel ... (READ CATEGORIES)

                          Extremely strong 1   24/
                          Very strong 2
                          Rather strong 3
                          Not too strong 4
                          Don't know 9

    C. Is there anything that <u>both</u> you and most (PEOPLE IN GROUP R HAS NAMED)
       <u>are not</u> getting a fair share of?

                          Yes . . . .(ASK D & E) . . . 1   25/
                          No . . . . (SKIP TO Q. 27) . . 2

    IF YES TO C:

    D. What is it? (IF NECESSARY, PROBE FOR THE MOST IMPORTANT ONE.)

                                                                   26-27/

    E. How strongly do you feel it is unfair or unjust that most (PEOPLE IN
       GROUP R HAS NAMED) are not getting a fair share of (WHATEVER R HAS
       NAMED)? Would you say you feel ... (READ CATEGORIES)

                          Extremely strong 1   28/
                          Very strong 2
                          Rather strong 3
                          Not too strong 4
                          Don't know 9

27. Last week, were you working full time, part time, going to school, keeping house
     or what? CIRCLE ONE CODE ONLY. IF MORE THAN ONE RESPONSE, GIVE PREFERENCE TO
     SMALLEST CODE NUMBER THAT APPLIES.

                    Working full time 1   29/
                    Working part time 2
                    With a job, but not at work because of tem
                       temporary illness, vacation, strike 3
                    Unemployed, laid off, looking for work 4
                    Retired 5
                    In school . . . . 6 ⎫ SKIP
                    Keeping house . . . . 7 ⎬ TO
                    Other (SPECIFY) _____ 8 ⎭ Q. 29

28. A. What kind of work do you (did you) normally do? That is, what (is/was) your
         job called?

              OCCUPATION: _____   30-32/

         IF IT'S NOT CLEAR FROM OCCUPATION NAME, ASK:
         What (do/did) you actually do in that job? Tell me, what (are/were)
         some of your main duties?

         _____

         ASK THIS ONLY IF OCCUPATION NAME IS NOT CLEAR AND IF YOU NEED MORE INFORMATION:
         What kind of place (do/did) you work for?

              INDUSTRY: _____   33-34/

         IF NOT CLEAR, ASK:
         What (do/did) they (make or do)?

         _____

     B. (a) Is your spouse working?
                              Yes 1   DECK 3
                              No 2   Cols. 74-76
                              NA 8   77-78

         (b) What kind of work (does/did) (he/she) normally do? What is the job called?

              OCCUPATION: _____

         (c) ONLY IF NOT CLEAR, ASK: What (does/did) (he/she) actually do on the job?

              _____

              What kind of place (is/was) it?

              _____

         (d) (Is/Was) it full time or part time?
                              Full time 1
                              Part time 2

29. Into which of these groups did your (and your spouse's) total income, from
     all sources, fall last year--1975--before taxes, that is? Just tell me the
     letter.

HAND CARD E	A. Under $1,000	01	35-36/
	B. $ 1,000 to 2,999	02	
	C. $ 3,000 to 3,999	03	
	D. $ 4,000 to 4,999	04	
	E. $ 5,000 to 5,999	05	
	F. $ 6,000 to 6,999	06	
	G. $ 7,000 to 7,999	07	
	H. $ 8,000 to 9,999	08	
	I. $10,000 to 14,999	09	
	J. $15,000 to 19,999	10	
	K. $20,000 to 24,999	11	
	L. $25,000 to 29,999	12	
	M. $30,000 to 39,999	13	
	N. $40,000 to 59,999	14	
	O. $60,000 to 79,999	15	
	P. $80,000 to 100,000	16	
	Q. Over $100,000	17	
	Refused	18	
	Don't know	98	

A. IF RESPONDENT LIVES WITH PARENTS OR IF RESPONDENT IS ELDERLY AND LIVES
    WITH CHILDREN, ASK: What do you estimate is your parents' (or children's)
    total income? ENTER CODE FROM ABOVE HERE: _____   DECK 1 78-79/

---

30. At any time since you left school have you been unemployed and looking
     for work for as long as a month?

                                      Yes 1   37/

                                      No 2

---

31. Have you ever--because of sickness, unemployment, or any other reasons--
     received anything like welfare, unemployment insurance, or other aid from
     government agencies?
                                      Yes . (ASK A & B) . 1   38/

                                      No 2

     IF YES:

     A. What did you receive?
                          Welfare 1   39/

                          Unemployment compensation 2

                          Other (SPECIFY) _____ 3

                          Social Security 4

     B. About how long did (have) you receive(d) it?

                                            _____ 40-41/

32. What is your religious preference? Is it Protestant, Catholic, Jewish, some other religion, or no religion?

                              Protestant . . . . (ASK A) 1   42/
                              Catholic 2
                              Jewish 3
                              None 4
                              Other (SPECIFY) _____ 5

    A. IF PROTESTANT: What specific denomination is that, if any?
                              Baptist 1   43/
                              Methodist 2
                              Lutheran 3
                              Presbyterian 4
                              Episcopalian 5
                              Other (SPECIFY) _____ 6

---

33. How often do you attend religious services? (USE CATEGORIES AS PROBES, IF NECESSARY)

                              Never 0   44/
                              Once a year 1
                              Several times a year . 2
                              At least once a month . 3
                              At least once a week . 4

---

34. Generally speaking, do you usually think of yourself as a Republican, a Democrat, an Independent, or what?

                              Republican . . . . (ASK A) . . . 1   45/
                              Democrat . . . . . (ASK A) . . . 2
                              Independent . . . (ASK B) . . . 3
                              Other (SPECIFY) _____ 4
                              No preference . . . (ASK B) . . . 5
                              Don't know 8

    A. IF REPUBLICAN OR DEMOCRAT: Would you call yourself a strong (Republican/Democrat) or not a very strong (Republican/Democrat)?
                              Strong 1   46/
                              Not very strong 2
                              Don't know 8

    B. IF INDEPENDENT OR NO PREFERENCE: Do you think of yourself as closer to the Republican or to the Democrat party?
                              Republican 1   47/
                              Democrat 2
                              Neither 3
                              Don't know 8

35. The seven numbers on this card go from "extremely liberal" (point 1) to "extremely conservative" (point 7). Which number best describes your political views?

    | HAND |
    | CARD |
    | F |

    EXTREMELY   EXTREMELY
    LIBERAL   CONSERVATIVE

    1   2   3   4   5   6   7   48/

36. In general, do you think the federal government is spending too much, too little, or about the right amount on social welfare programs?

    Too little 1   49/

    About right 2

    Too much 3

    Don't know 8

37. How successful do you think the government is at getting help to those most in need of it? Would you say it's very successful, somewhat successful, not too successful, or not at all successful?

    Very successful 1   50/

    Somewhat successful 2

    Not too successful 3

    Not at all successful . . . 4

    Don't know 8

Thank you very much for your time and cooperation. May I have your telephone number in case my supervisor wants to check my work?

TELEPHONE NUMBER: _____

INTERVIEWER: _____   DATE: _____

TIME
INTERVIEW   [:]   AM
ENDED: PM

51-78/Word Pairs

80/5

APPENDIX 2
DELIBERATE CONFOUNDING PLAN

The reduction in treatments-per-respondent from 64 vignettes to only eight could not be accomplished without some costs in reliability of measurement. Since each respondent experienced only one-eighth of the full range of treatment combinations, in the analysis of certain higher-order interaction effects, it becomes impossible to distinguish between three possible causes of variation in a specific respondent's level of support. First, and most obvious, are the specific characteristics of the disadvantaged person described in any given vignette—i.e., the level of poverty and disability, the character's age, and the apparent cause for the problems depicted. These, of course, are our experimental variables, which may act independently or may interact in any number of ways to produce patterns of support for a vignette character. Second, there may be some effects on level of support which follow from a particular grouping of eight treatment combinations into a "treatment package." That is, the level of support for a vignette character may be due in part to the juxtaposition of that vignette with other particular vignettes in its package, as well as to the specific circumstances surrounding that character, with level of support either elevated or depressed as a result of the contrast with other vignettes in the package. This artificial source of variation in support will be called the *protocol effect*. Third, there may be *order effects* due to the sequence of treatment combinations within the package of eight vignettes administered to any respondent. For example, level of support might grow or decay because of respondent learning or respondent fatigue.

Thus, when a single respondent is assigned to a treatment package or protocol which comprises less than all possible treatment combinations, the substantive causes for the level of support for a vignette character must be confounded (for that respondent) with either order effects or protocol effects. To see why, consider the analysis of the results from a far simpler experiment—a two by two factorial with only "age of victim" and "cause of plight" as the two-level experimental factors. There are four possible treatment combinations:

(1) young—self-caused
(2) old—self-caused
(3) young—other-caused
(4) old—other-caused.

First, let us assume that there is no difficulty in exposing any subject-respondent to *all four* treatment combinations: In the terminology used above, there are no *protocol* effects to be concerned with. If we are interested in examining the interaction effect between age of victim and causality, then we will be giving attention to the level of support measured for each of the four cells in our two by two design. Any source of variation in level of support for any of the treatment combinations other than the treatment itself would thus prejudice our ability to estimate the actual effects of any given combination of factor levels on level of support. Now if we were to assign the four treatments to our respondents *always in the same order*—say, 1, 2, 3, 4—we would have no way to tell how much of the support measured for treatment 1 was due to the causal influence of the experimental factors and how much was due to the fact that it was the *first* of the treatments to be experienced by respondents. This difficulty can be simply overcome, however, by *balancing the order* of the four treatments over all the respondents, that is, by insuring that each of the treatment combinations appears an equal number of times in each ordinal position. In order to eliminate the bias of *ordinal position only*, it is necessary merely to provide for *four* kinds of treatment package, in which each of the treatment combinations occupies each of the four possible ordinal positions. For example, the set

(a) 1, 2, 3, 4
(b) 4, 1, 2, 3
(c) 3, 4, 1, 2
(d) 2, 3, 4, 1

satisfies this requirement. Note, however, that balancing the order of treatment combinations increases the number of subject-respondents needed for the experiment *by a factor of 4*, since each of the four sets must be presented to an equal number of respondents (in order to skirt some potentially serious problems in analysis of results).

If, to go even further, we wished to eliminate any possible bias due to the full sequential order of the four treatment combinations in the set, we would have to provide 4! = 24 different treatment packages, thereby increasing the number of respondents required by a factor of 24. Fortunately, experience shows that the biases likely to be introduced by the entire sequence of treatments are likely to be negligible in applications like this one, so that balancing the ordinal position of treatments should be sufficient correction for the confident analysis of interaction effects.

Now let us complicate the matter somewhat by adding the restriction that only two of the four treatment combinations may be presented to any respondent. This raises the problem that the level of support for any treatment combination may be in part determined by its juxtaposition in a treatment package with some other particular treatment combination, as well as by the treatment combination itself— i.e., the *protocol* effect described above. Disregarding the problem of treatment order for the moment, we now have a total of six treatment sets or protocols: 1 with 2; 1 with 3; 1 with 4; 2 with 3; 2 with 4; and 3 with 4. With two possible treatment orders within each protocol, we thus have 12 different protocols necessary to implement the two by two design. In order to examine the two variable interaction between age and cause, we must use equal numbers of each protocol in the experiment, thereby increasing the number of respondents required by a factor of 12—a potentially expensive proposition.

The implications of this small example for our study should be clear enough. Our complex experimental design contained 64 possible treatment combinations. To reduce the number of treatments per respondent to a reasonable level—say, fewer than ten—while keeping *every* respondent's support measurement free from the confounding effects of protocol and ordinal position would have required something in the order of four billion respondents. Since we were constrained to keep the total number of respondents in the vicinity of 400, it immediately became apparent that we would have to permit the confounding of experimental, order and protocol effects for some of the two, three and four variable interactions as the price of reducing the number of treatments per respondent. However, by designing the experiment in *two* entirely separate replications and systematically planning both the grouping of vignettes into protocols and the sequencing of vignettes within protocols, we were able to insure that the interaction components which were confounded in one replication would be free from this problem in the other. The actual interactions that were confounded in each replication are outlined in Table 1 of this appendix.

The confounding procedure raises some minor difficulties for analysis. In computing sums of squares (for analysis of variance) due to interactions in which there are some confounded components, only half of the sample (i.e., the unconfounded replication) will have scores that can be used in the calculations. In all, 28 interaction components were confounded—14 in each replication. In each replication, seven components were confounded with protocol effects while the remaining seven were confounded with order effects. Plainly, planned confounding of this kind entails some loss of statistical power, and the detection of significant interaction effects may be impeded by the reductions in cell size inherent in the design. The analysis in Chapter 5 reveals, however, that this loss of power caused us no serious difficulty in detecting differences in support levels or trends in higher-order interactions. In fact, many interactions which were significant at the .05 level involved differences in mean support scores of far too small a magnitude to have consequences for policy decisions. For this reason, we imposed the additional requirement in that chapter that measured effects had to account for at least 1 percent (rounded) of the variance in our dependent support variable to be included in the discussion.

In summary, our deliberate, systematic confounding plan allows us to reduce vastly the number of treatments-per-respondent and still attain unbiased estimates of all effects with at least half the number of cases in the sample. Some interaction effects were estimated with less precision, but this loss of precision seems to have had little practical consequence, since we found ourselves with an embarrassing *surfeit* of statistically significant interactions rather than a paucity.

To read Table 1 requires first learning the letter system of notation outlined in the first third of the table. The next third indicates the effects of interest which we want to separate out from the confounding effects of protocol and ordinal position. The point to be noted is that the confounded interactions are different for each replication and that if an effect is confounded for one-half of the sample, it is not confounded for the other half. Thus, every interaction of interest can be tested, even if with a reduced sample.

Each vignette contributes to the sum of squares for all main effects and some interaction terms. For example, the second-order interaction of level of poverty, age of victim, and cause of problem (poverty by age by cause) involves the contrast of all vignettes depicting characters with

(1) low poverty, no disability, old age, and other-caused problems (AEF);

(2) high acute poverty, no disability, old age, and other-caused problems (BEF);

(3) high chronic poverty, no disability, old age, and other-caused problems (ABEF)

with all other vignettes. If any of the above three type of vignettes were intentionally confounded with protocol or order effects in either replication (half-sample), support scores from those cases could not be used in calculating the appropriate sum of squares. By consulting Table 1, we learn that vignettes of this first type—encoded "AEF"—are confounded with order effects in replication 2. Consequently, only scores from cases in replication 1 are available for computing this component of the poverty by age by causality interaction sum of squares. Similarly, vignettes of the second type—encoded "BEF"—are confounded with protocol effects in replication 1, so that only responses from cases in replication 2 may be used in computing the sum of squares for that component. Likewise, the third type of vignette (ABEF in Table 1), is confounded with order effects in replication 1, so that, again, only half the cases are usable in the computation. The following list of effects provides a breakdown of all interactions into their respective components using the codes in the legend of Table 1. The reader need only consult that table to determine which interaction term components were calculated using only half of the sample.

Table 1:   Deliberate Confounding Plan

A. Description of Levels

Levels of poverty	*	=	no poverty
	A	=	low poverty
	B	=	high acute poverty
	AB	=	high chronic poverty
Level of disability	*	=	no disability
	C	=	low disability
	D	=	high acute disability
	CD	=	high chronic disability
Age of victim	*	=	young victim
	E	=	old victim
Cause of problem	*	=	self-caused
	F	=	other-caused

Note: * denotes no letter for factor level in component code

B. List of Effects

Main effects
    Level of poverty (A, B, AB)
    Level of disability (C, D, CD)
    Age of victim (E)
    Cause of problem (F)

First-order interactions
    Poverty by disability (AC, AD, ACD, BC, BD, BCD, ABC, ABD, ABCD)
    Poverty by age (AE, BE, ABE)

Table 1:   Deliberate Confounding Plan (Cont)

Poverty by cause (AF, BF, ABF)
Disability by age (CE, DE, CDE)
Disability by cause (CF, DF, CDF)
Age by cause (EF)

Second-order interactions
Poverty by disability by age (ACE, ADE, ACDE, BCE, BDE, BCDE
ABCE, ABDE, ABCDE)
Poverty by disability by cause (ACF, ADF, ACDF, BCF, BDF, BCDF,
ABCF, ABDF, ABCDF)
Poverty by age by cause (AEF, BEF, ABEF)
Disability by age by cause (CEF, DEF, CDEF)

Third-order interactions
Poverty by disability by age by cause
(ACEF, ADEF, ACDEF, BCEF, BDEF, BCDEF, ABCEF, ABCDEF)

C. Confounded Interactions

(1) Interaction components confounded in replication 1

Confounded with

Protocol effect	Order effect
ABCF	ABCDE
ABDE	ABEF
ACE	ACF
ADF	AD
BCD	BCE
BEF	BDEF
CDEF	CDF

(2) Interaction components confounded in replication 2

Confounded with

Protocol effect	Order effect
ABC	ABCD
ABCDEF	ABDEF
ADE	AC
AF	AEF
BCDE	BCDEF
BCF	BD

REFERENCES

ALEXANDER, C. (1979) Social Work Month: March 1979. Washington, DC: National Association of Social Workers.

ALSTON, J. P. and I. K. DEAN (1972) "Socioeconomic factors associated with attitudes toward welfare recipients and the causes of poverty." Social Service Rev. 46: 13-23.

AXINN, J. and H. LEVIN (1975) Social Welfare. New York: Harper & Row.

BERKOWITZ, L. (1975) A Survey of Social Psychology. Hinsdale, IL: Dryden Press.

––– and D. H. CONNOR (1966) "Success, failure, and social responsibility." J. of Personality and Social Psychology. : 664-669.

BERKOWITZ, M., W. G. JOHNSON, E. H. MURPHY (1976) Public Policy Toward Disability. New York: Praeger.

BLAUSTEIN, A. I. (1978) "Proposition 13 = Catch 22." Harper's (November): 18-22.

BREMNER, R. H. (1956) From the Depths. New York: New York University Press.

BRIELAND, D., L. B. COSTIN, C. R. ATHERTON, and Contributors (1975) Contemporary Social Work: An Introduction to Social Work and Social Welfare. New York: McGraw-Hill.

BRYAN, J. G. and M. A. TEST (1967) "Models and helping: naturalistic studies in aiding behavior." J. of Personality and Social Psychology 6: 400-407.

BUTLER, R. R. (1975) Why Survive? Being Old in America. New York: Harper & Row.

CALIFANO, J. A. (1978) "Public input at HEW." J. of the Institute for Socioeconomic Studies 3: 1-8.

CANTRIL, H. (1965) The Pattern of Human Concerns. New Brunswick, NJ: Rutgers University Press.

CARTER, G. L. H. FIFIELD, and H. SHIELDS (1973) Public Attitudes Toward Welfare: An Opinion Poll. Los Angeles: Regional Research Institute in Social Welfare, University of Southern California.

COLL, B. (1969) Perspectives in Public Welfare. Washington, DC: U.S. Government Printing Office.

CONOVER, W. J. (1971) Practical Nonparametric Statistics. New York: John Wiley.

COOK, F. L. (1977) Differences in Public Support for Seven Social Welfare Groups: Description and Explanation. Doctoral dissertation, University of Chicago.

COOK, T. D. and D. T. CAMPBELL (1976) "The design and conduct of quasi-experiments in field settings," in M. Dunnette (ed.) Handbook of Organizational Psychology. Skokie, IL: Rand McNally.

Council of Economic Advisors (1979) Economic Report to Congress. Washington, DC: U.S. Government Printing Office.

CURTIN, R. T. and C. D. COWAN (1975) "Public attitudes toward fiscal programs," in B. Strumpel, C. Cowan, F. Juster, and J. Schmiedeskamp (eds.) Surveys of Consumers. Ann Arbor, MI: Institute for Social Research, University of Michigan.

DEAUX, K. (1976) The Behavior of Women and Men. Monterey, CA: Brooks/ Cole.

DERTHICK, M. (1975) Uncontrollable Spending for Social Services Grants. Washington, DC: Brookings Institution.

DUNCAN, O. D. (1975) Introduction to Structural Equation Models. New York: Academic Press.

ERSKINE, H. (1975) "The polls: government role in welfare." Public Opinion Q. 34: 251-274.

FEAGIN, J. R. (1975) Subordinating the Poor: Welfare and American Beliefs. Englewood Cliffs, NJ: Prentice-Hall.

FISHBEIN, M. and I. AJZEN (1975) Belief, Attitude, Intention, and Behavior: An Introduction to Theory and Research. Reading, MA: Addison-Wesley.

GILBERT, N. (1977a) "The transformation of social services." Social Service Rev. 51: 624-641.

GILBERT N. (1977b) "The burgeoning social service payload." Society 14: 63-65.

——— and H. SPECHT (1974) Dimensions of Social Welfare Policy. Englewood Cliffs, NJ: Prentice-Hall.

GONZALEZ, A. J. and J. WELLBORN (1979) "Proposition 13 fever." Social Work 24: 3-4.

GOODWIN, L. (1972a) Do the Poor Want to Work? A Social Psychological Study of Work Orientations. Washington, DC: Brookings Institution.

——— (1972b) "How suburban families view the work orientations of the welfare poor: problems in social stratification and social policy." Social Problems 19: 337-348.

GOULDNER, A. W. (1960) "The norm of reciprocity: a preliminary statement." Amer. Soc. Rev. 25: 161-178.

HANBACH, J. (1974) Will Student Nurses Devalue an "Innocent" Patient? A Study of the Just World Hypothesis in the Health Services Area. Master's thesis, Northwestern University.

Harris, L. and Associates (1975) The Myth and Reality of Aging in America. Washington, DC: National Council on the Aging.

——— (1978) Study Number P383T. (Available from Harris, 630 Fifth Avenue, New York, 10020.)

Hecht Institute (1977) Finding Federal Money for Children's Services. Washington, DC: Child Welfare League of America.

HEISE, D. R. (1975) Causal Analysis. New York: John Wiley.

HOROWITZ, I. A. (1968) "Effect of choice and locus of dependence on helping behavior." J. of Personality and Social Psychology 8: 373-376.

KAHN, A. J. (1973) Social Policy and Social Services. New York: Random House.

KATONA, G. (1974) American Attitudes Toward Fiscal Programs and Taxation. Ann Arbor, MI: Survey Research Center, University of Michigan.

――― (1975) Psychological Economics. New York: Elsevier.

KELMAN, H. C. (1974) "Attitudes are alive and well and gainfully employed in the sphere of action." Amer. Psychologist 33: 310-324.

KREBS, D. L. (1970) "Altruism: an examination of the concept and a review of the literature." Psych. Bull. 73: 258-302.

LAUER, R. H. (1971) "The middle class looks at poverty." Urban and Social Change Rev. 5: 8-10.

LERNER, M. J. (1965) "Evaluation of performance as a function of performer's reward and attentiveness." J. of Personality and Social Psychology 5: 355-360.

――― (1970) "The desire for justice and reactions to victims," in J. Macaulay and L. Berkowitz (eds.) Altruism and Helping Behavior. New York: Academic Press.

――― and C. SIMMONS (1966) "Observers' reaction to the 'innocent' victim." J. of Personality and Social Psychology 4: 203-210.

MACAROV, D. (1978) The Design of Social Welfare. New York: Holt, Rinehart & Winston.

McFARLAND, D. D. (1977) "The aged in the 21st century: a demographic view," in L. F. Jarvik (ed.) The Long Tomorrow: Aging into the 21st Century. New York: Gardner Press.

McNEMAR, Q. (1969) Psychological Statistics. New York: John Wiley.

MAYNES, C. W. (1974) "U.S. and the world: whole new ball game." Chicago Sun-Times, Viewpoint Section (December 1): 1-2.

MELEMED, B. B. (1976) Making Title XX Work. Washington, DC: National Council on Aging.

MILLER, A. H. (1978) "Will public attitudes defeat welfare reform?" Public Welfare 36: 48-54.

MILLER, W. E. and D. STOKES (1963) "Constituency influence in congress." Amer. Pol. Sci. Rev. 57: 45-56.

MORRIS, R. (1979) Social Policy of the American Welfare State. New York: Harper & Row.

MUELLER, E. (1963) "Public attitudes toward fiscal programs." Q. J. of Economics 77: 210-235.

MUELLER, C. (1977) Child Advocates Checklist. Washington, DC: Hecht Institute, Child Welfare League of America.

National Council on Aging (1978) Fact Book on Aging: A Profile of America's Older Population. Washington, DC: National Council on Aging.

New York Times (1979) "Scrutinizing priorities that shaped the budget." New York Times (January 28): E 3.

NIE, N. H., S. VERBA and J. H. PETROCIK (1976) The Changing American Voter. Cambridge, MA: Harvard University Press.

OWEN, H. and C. L. SCHULTZE (1976) Setting National Priorities: The Next

Ten Years. Washington, DC: Brookings Institution.

RUBIN, Z. and L. A. PEPLAU (1973) "Belief in a just world and reactions to another's lot: a study of participants in the national draft lottery." J. of Social Issues 29: 73-93.

——— (1975) "Who believes in a just world?" J. of Social Issues 31: 65-90.

RYTINA, J. H., W. H. FORM and J. PEASE (1970) "Income and stratification ideology: beliefs about the american opportunity structure." Amer. J. of Sociology 75: 703-716.

SAMUELSON, P. (1976) Economics. New York: McGraw-Hill.

SCHILTZ, M. E. (1970) Public Attitudes Toward Social Security, 1935-1965. Washington, DC: U.S. Government Printing Office.

SCHWARTZ, S. (1975) "The justice of need and the activation of humanitarian norms." J. of Social Issues 31: 111-136.

SHANAS, E. (1962) The Health of Older People: A Social Survey. Cambridge, MA: Harvard University Press.

SHOPLER, J. and M. W. MATTHEWS (1965) The influence of the perceived causal locus of partner's dependence on the use of interpersonal power." J. of Personality and Social Psychology 2: 609-612.

STEIN, B. (1971) On Relief: The Economics of Poverty and Public Welfare. New York: Basic Books.

TAYLOR, D. G. (1975) National Priorities: Social Welfare Programs. Manuscript, National Opinion Research Center, University of Chicago.

U.S. Bureau of the Census (1978) Money Income in 1976 of Families and Persons in the United States. Current Population Reports Series P-60, Number 114. Washington, DC: U.S. Government Printing Office.

U.S. General Accounting Office (1977) Report to the Congress: Home Health— the Need for a National Policy to Provide for the Elderly. Washington, DC: U.S. Government Printing Office.

——— (1978) Will Federal Assistance to California Be Affected by Proposition 13? Washington, DC: U.S. Government Printing Office.

WALSTER, E. (1966) "Assignment of responsibility for an accident." J. of Personality and Social Psychology 3: 73-79.

WHITE, G. F. and J. E. HAAS (1975) Assessment of Research on National Disasters. Cambridge, MA: MIT Press.

WILLIAMSON, J. B. (1974a) "Beliefs about the welfare poor." Sociology and Social Research 58: 163-175.

——— (1974b) "Beliefs about the motivation of the poor and attitudes toward poverty policy." Social Problems 21: 634-648.

——— (1974c) "The stigma of public dependency: a comparison of alternative forms of public aid to the poor." Social Problems 22: 213-228.

WOODROOFE, K. (1962) From Charity to Social Work in England and the United States. Toronto: University of Toronto Press.

ZUCKERMAN, K. B., R. S. KRAVITZ and L. WHEELER (1974) The Belief in a Just World and Reactions to Innocent Victims. Manuscript.

INDEX

223

ABOUT THE AUTHOR

FAY LOMAX COOK has been an assistant professor at the Center for Urban Affairs and the School of Education, Northwestern University, since 1979. From 1975 to 1979, she was an assistant professor at the Loyola University of Chicago School of Social Work. She was a study director at the National Opinion Research Center, University of Chicago, and received her Ph.D. at the University of Chicago School of Social Service Administration in 1977. Articles by Dr. Cook have been published in the *Social Service Review*, the *Gerontologist*, Leonard Rutman's *Evaluation Research Methods*, and Emilio Viano's *Victims and Society*.